# Betting F

# 2015

MW00911923

## www.BettingBaseball.net

# Betting Baseball 2015

## www.BettingBaseball.net

---

## RICHARD NICHOLS

---

*The race is not always to the swift nor the battle to the strong, but that's the way to bet.*

*Damon Runyon*

Questions, comments, additional information, and possible corrections can be found at BettingBaseball.net. Earlier versions of Betting Baseball, and much of this current work, was written and is copyrighted by Michael Murray.

All Rights reserved. No part of this publication may be reproduced, stored in a retrieval system, or transmitted by any means, electronic, mechanical, photocopying, or otherwise, without the prior written permission of the writer.

Copyright 2015

# CONTENTS

# BETTING BASEBALL

Betting baseball is simple. Just pick the winner. There are no point spreads to beat, and the reduced juice seems to be a gift. It is never that easy, however. Baseball is the most draining, exhausting sport to bet. From February to October, it is constantly in the news. The season doesn't start in April; it begins during spring training when the optimism of every team permeates the landscape. Bettors fall prey to the same optimism. They spend all March listening to the talking heads and other self-proclaimed baseball experts. They do plenty of due diligence, never thinking that much of what they hear and read is simply noise rather than news. They know the hot pitchers coming out of spring training, have read what "unnamed scouts" are saying, and collect tiny pieces of information from coaches, managers and reporters that foretell how successful a team will be in the upcoming season.

In theory, this is all good. In practice, danger is always around the corner. All teams have agendas. Some want to sell more tickets. Some want to bump up a player's trade value. Or sometimes a simple decision is rethought. A player who won his job in 75 spring training at-bats against suspect competition will lose his job once his first slump hits. Misinformation is commonplace in baseball. A bettor can think he knows enough, and think he knows how a game will play out, but in the end, the uncertainties carry the day. I have listed below some key points to surviving and prospering during the baseball season. Above all, common sense should rule the day:

- Money management means minimal exposure of your bankroll.
- If your line is vastly different from the market line, you are wrong. Re-check your work.
- Spread the risk; betting five games at 2% of your bankroll is far less risky than one game at 10%.
- Bet no more than you can afford to lose.
- Don't chase your losses.

- Winning isn't everything; if you can't enjoy a great baseball game because you had money on the losing side, you might be betting too much on the game.
- Don't bet parlays. While a sharp bettor can find an edge in some parlays, winning a parlay may harm your money management skills later in the season. Keep it as simple as possible.
- Ignore your hunches.
- Don't vary your wager size by more than 50%. If your average wager is 2% of bankroll, keep your maximum bet at 3%.
- Locks are a myth. If a number looks way off, chances are you overlooked something the bookmaker hasn't.
- Review both your winning and losing bets. While it is important to understand why you lose, it is equally important to understand why you won.
- Don't be stupid.
- Don't be greedy.
- Keep a cool head.
- Understand that you have no control over what happens in a game. Once you play it, forget it. If winning or losing is so important to you regardless of the amount wagered, don't watch the game.
- Don't let the thrill of victory or the agony of defeat affect your next play.
- You are never as good as you think you are when you are hot, nor as bad as you think you are when you are cold.
- Be satisfied with any profit.
- Concern yourself more with what happens in the game than the outcome. Teams that dominate a game will often lose. In the long run, it is better to be right and lose than be wrong and win.
- Make your own line, and understand how the bookmaker makes his.
- Keep in mind that you will lose 10 games in a row at some point in the season, particularly if you play a good number of underdogs.
- Never get tired of other people's opinions.
- Never put too much stock in other people's opinions.

- Keep in mind that the line is the sum total of the ignorance of the betting public. Never overestimate the general public's ability to pick winners.
- Without discipline, there is no profit in gambling.

Money management is a defensive tactic in betting. It keeps you alive to bet again. Every day a bettor is going to see lines that look too good to be true. Without a system of risk control, that bettor is going to have problems surviving the losing streaks that are inevitable in baseball. The percentage of sports bettors that profit, long-term, is estimated at 1-3%. That is only an estimate, but it is 100% true that few people are making money on sports betting. It requires a lot of discipline and hard work. Intelligence helps as well, but a working knowledge of math should be enough if a bettor is disciplined and willing to work.

Probability rules baseball. Who wins or loses is secondary. If a coin landing on heads pays +110, is there any doubt which side you should bet? The ultimate goal of each baseball bettor should be to find these coin toss situations with the odds in his favor. Success in this guarantees success in betting. Mike Caro calls these the absolute truths of probability:

- You must eventually lose if the odds are against you.
- You must eventually win if the odds are in your favor.
- If skill affects the odds in any way, then skillful players will eventually fare better than unskilled players.

Putting the odds in your favor involves having a good process when betting baseball. A bettor should have a solid understanding of mathematics, a deep intelligence of the game, the willingness to use statistics, understand the principles of probability, and develop a plan of action that will ensure survival when the inevitable losing streak hits. A winning bettor is aware that the frequency of winning is not important; the frequency multiplied by the payout is what matters. Michael Mauboussim, an investment banker for First Boston, describes an investment matrix that looks like this:

|  | GOOD OUTCOME | BAD OUTCOME |
|---|---|---|
| GOOD PROCESS | Deserved Success | Bad Luck |
| BAD PROCESS | Dumb Luck | Poetic Justice |

In the long run, it is better to lose sharp than it is to win stupid. When you are making around ten plays a day for nearly 200 days, it is how well you play the game that really matters. Dumb Luck may win out over a period of time, but Poetic Justice is always lurking behind the corner.

So how does one know when one's process was correct, and it wasn't just dumb luck that led to the win (or bad luck that led to the loss)? The simplest way to tell is to compare the closing line of the game with the line you bet. If you went 0-5 with your bets but beat the closing lines in all five games, your process was likely solid. It just didn't work out.

Of course, too many of those "right side loser" games will knock you out of the game before you can reap the rewards of a good process. That is when money management becomes a key factor. Money management should be simple. A bettor should set his base bankroll each season, adjusting once that bankroll increases or decreases 10%. If you like to bet many games, keep the base unit low (1% range). It is a clinical approach to sports betting and money management. It is cool, efficient, and the most mathematically viable.

If you only bet a few games a day, or consider gambling a hobby using only your disposable income, a higher percentage of your bankroll can be justified. The cost of busting out is simply waiting until a few paydays come around.

There are other, more sophisticated money management systems out there. The Kelly Criterion is one of the more popular ones. Kelly is a complicated, aggressive system designed to maximize profit. Wikipedia.com describes the formula below:

$$f^* = \frac{bp - q}{b},$$

*Where*
*f\* is the fraction of the current bankroll to wager;*
*b is the odds received on the wager;*
*p is the probability of winning;*
*q is the probability of losing, which is 1 − p.*

As an example, if a gamble has a 40% chance of winning (p = 0.40, q = 0.60), but the gambler receives 2-to-1 odds on a winning bet (b = 2), then the gambler should bet 10% of the bankroll at each opportunity (f\* = 0.10), in order to maximize the long-run growth rate of the bankroll.

The Kelly Criterion boils down to this: the bigger your edge, the bigger your bet. It is a high risk, high reward method designed to maximize profits for a sports bettor. Using Kelly, a bettor has a 50% chance of losing half his payroll at some point. He has a 30% chance of losing 30% of his payroll.

Most bettors who follow the Kelly Criterion use variations of the method. Half Kelly is a dialed down version of the formula that lowers the risk to bettors. A 55% handicapper using half Kelly will have his average wager at 2.8% bankroll. In baseball, with the daily grind and thousands of betting chances over the course of a season, that is too high for most. Unless you have the experience and knowledge to know your true edge, it is best to avoid using variations of the Kelly Criterion.

In the long run, however, the greatest money management system in the world doesn't matter if the bettor is playing a negative expectation game. Work on your sports betting first, then worry about more complicated money management later.

# The Martingale System

On occasion, a bettor will run across a fellow degenerate who wants to discuss some type of Martingale System. Martingale is one of the oldest betting systems using a negative progression. It is named after Henry Martingale, an English casino owner in the 1700s who advised gamblers to chase their losing wagers with even bigger bets.

This system is very simple. Keep betting until you win. Double each losing bet. As long as you win a bet, you will continue to bet at your initial level. When you lose, you will move up to the next wager, doubling the amount of the previous wager. Use of the system ensures that whenever your wager eventually wins, you will win the amount of the original wager. No matter how unlucky one is, he is bound to eventually win at least one bet.

The theory behind the system may be sound given an infinite bankroll, but the reality certainly isn't. A $100 Martingale bettor who has lost five even money bets in a row will be betting $1600 to win $100. If the coin flip has gone against him 10 times, that bettor has to bet $102,400 to win his initial $100 back.

That obviously is impossible. Sportsbooks don't take that high of bets, and sports bettors who use Martingale wouldn't have that much money even if they found a sportsbook willing to take his action.

# THE SEARCH FOR BULLSHIT

Joe Posnanski once interviewed Bill James about what made him tick. Now 65 years old and safely embedded in the inner-circle of the Boston Red Sox, James is still fighting the fight against conventional wisdom and "bullshit".

"Bullshit has tremendous advantages over knowledge. Bullshit can be created as needed, on demand, without limit. Anything that happens, you can make up an explanation for why it happened.

"There was a Kansas football game a year ago; some Texas-based football team, much better than Kansas, came to Lawrence and struggled through the first quarter — KU with, like, a 7-3 lead at the end of the first quarter. The rest of the game, KU lost, like, 37-0, or something. The announcer had an immediate explanation for it: The Texas team flew in the day before, they spent the night sleeping in a strange hotel; it takes them a while to get their feet on the ground.

"It's pure bullshit, of course, but he was paid to say that ... if it had happened the other way, and KU had lost the first quarter, 24-0, and then 'won' the rest of the game 17-14 (thus losing 38-17) ... if that had happened, we both know that the announcer would have had an immediate explanation for why THAT had happened. ... Bullshit is without limit."

Bullshit is best defined as a summary opinion without evidence. James began writing in 1977 and has written more than twenty books devoted to baseball history, statistics, and stamping out the bullshit. Many baseball bettors grew up listening to the likes of Joe Morgan and Tim McCarver spout off conventional wisdom like a Saudi Arabian oil well gushes black gold. The bettors take those clichés taught in their wasted youth and try to turn that knowledge into money. "I'll bet on him. He just knows how to win," says conventional wisdom when a mediocre pitcher rides a solid offense and good fortune to 20 wins. "

A winning gambler should make it his goal to profit from the bullshit. Skepticism is required in all things. When the line is Kansas City -130, one must question why. One must try to prove that number "wrong" using solid techniques and unbiased numbers. The gambler will fail to prove that number wrong most of the time (by wrong, I mean off far enough to make a bet).

However, the concept remains. We must assume bullshit at the line because we don't know what line is "true" and what isn't until we examine it. The tools listed in this book will help a beginning gambler apply this skepticism. Can one ever know if the line is accurate? No, there are too many variables involved in knowing a team's actual likelihood of winning a single ballgame.

We don't need to be accurate, however. We just need to be better than the conventional wisdom (the line). People once thought the earth was flat. People also once thought the earth was spherical. Both are wrong, but one is more wrong than the other. Our goal is to think the earth is spherical while the sportsbook believes the earth is flat.

# BASICS OF BETTING BASEBALL

The typical baseball line looks like this at a sports book:

| | TEAM | PITCHER | RUN LN | MONEY LN | TOTAL | |
|---|---|---|---|---|---|---|
| 911 | Giants | Vogelsong | +1.5 -184 | +105 | OVER 7 | -116 |
| 912 | Padres | Kennedy | -1.5 +198 | -113 | UNDER 7 | +106 |

This line says:

- The top team, San Francisco, is the visiting team.
- The bottom team, San Diego, is the home team.
- Ryan Vogelsong is starting for the Rockies.
- Ian Kennedy is starting for the Padres.
- The Giants plus 1.5 runs is –1.84.
- San Diego minus 1.5 runs is +1.98.
- San Francisco is a +105 underdog.
- The Padres are a –113 favorite.
- Over 7 is a –116 favorite.
- Under 7 is a +106 underdog.

The line also gives a few more details. The sports book is using a dime line on the Total, meaning that there is a 10-cent difference between the dog and the favorite. They also use it on the Run Line. Most sportsbooks use a 20-cent line when offering Run Lines and Totals; action on Totals is usually sharper and the book tries to minimize its risk.

The sports book listed above doesn't have this fear. On the money line above you see an 18-cent difference between the favorite and dogs. This sports book (Pinnaclesports.com) uses an 8-cent line on the money line that graduates upward as the price of the favorite increases. For example, two evenly matched teams might each have a –104 line to win the game outright. If one team is a heavy favorite, then that 8-cent spread will be larger.

Most quality books use a dime line; this has been standard practice since a Las Vegas book decided to attract customers by lowering its juice. Other books were forced to discount their vig to meet this competition, and baseball bettors have been spoiled ever since. Baseball doesn't generate much positive revenue for books, particularly compared to football. The dime line is a major reason.

One aspect a bettor needs to know is the concept of listing pitchers when making wagers. Sportsbooks take the above bet not as San Francisco vs. San Diego but as Vogelsong vs. Kennedy. If either pitcher doesn't start the game, the bet is cancelled and wager refunded.

To avoid this, an "action bet" can be placed by the bettor. Action means a bettor will keep his bet regardless of any pitching changes. The sports book will readjust the payout odds, but the bettor will still have his wager. For example, if Vogelsong can't make his start and is replaced by Madison Bumgarner, the Giants may be a -140 favorite. The action bettor who originally had San Francisco +105 now has San Francisco -140.

It is usually a mistake to request an "action" wager. It can be done on occasion. I may use action when I know I will be unable to re-bet my wager and am betting against a team more than against a starting pitcher. However, a starting pitcher has too much of an impact on the game to risk money on this unknown factor. Action bets also mean you are stuck with a book's readjustment. This eliminates the ability to line-shop for value.

# A SPORTSBOOK'S HOLD PERCENTAGE

To see the effect of the dime line on a sports book, one must be familiar with the theoretical hold percentage (THP). THP is what a book expects to make under perfect conditions per $100 bet. In sports using point spreads, the THP is 4.55% assuming the book uses the standard bet 11 to win 10. Baseball is a bit trickier; the THP changes depending on the odds. The formula for THP is:

| Step 1 |               | 1 – (1 + Dog Price)   |
|--------|---------------|-----------------------|
| Step 2 | Multiplied by | (1 + Favorite Price)  |
| Step 3 | Divided by    | 1 + Dog Price         |
| Step 4 | Multiplied by | Favorite Price        |
| Step 5 | Plus          | 1                     |
| Step 6 | Plus          | Favorite Price        |

The THP is also expressed as:

$$1 - (1+\text{Dog Price}) * (1+\text{Favorite Price}) \text{ divided by}$$
$$((1 + \text{Dog Price}) * \text{Favorite Price} + 1 + \text{Favorite Price})$$

Here is Pinnacle's THP with a +196 underdog facing off against a -214 favorite:

$$\text{THP} = 1 - (1+1.96) * (1+2.14) / ((1+1.96) * 2.14 + 1 + 2.14)$$

The THP=1.90%. If there is $10,000 wagered on this game perfectly split with no line movements necessary, Pinnacle will hold $190.

A sportsbook like Pinnacle needs heavy volume if it is going make baseball profitable to the house. One sports book goes a bit further than even Pinnacle. 5Dimes.com offers a five-cent line on overnight wagers. There is a $500 per game limit on bets to protect the book from sophisticated bettors, but lines like that give unprecedented value to the recreational gambler. Below is a table detailing the THP for a sports book with a nickel line:

| 5-CENT THP | DOG PRICE | FAV PRICE | BOOK EARN ON 30K |
|---|---|---|---|
| 1.20% | +1.00 | -1.05 | $361 |
| 1.10% | +1.10 | -1.15 | $328 |
| 1.00% | +1.20 | -1.25 | $300 |
| 0.92% | +1.30 | -1.35 | $274 |
| 0.84% | +1.40 | -1.45 | $252 |
| 0.78% | +1.50 | -1.55 | $233 |

Pinnacle's 8-cent line THP is listed below: After –1.90, the line breaks into a dime line.

| 8-CENT THP | DOG PRICE | FAV PRICE | BOOK EARN ON 30K |
|---|---|---|---|
| 1.89% | +1.00 | -1.08 | $566 |
| 1.72% | +1.10 | -1.18 | $515 |
| 1.57% | +1.20 | -1.28 | $470 |
| 1.44% | +1.30 | -1.38 | $432 |
| 1.33% | +1.40 | -1.48 | $397 |
| 1.23% | +1.50 | -1.58 | $367 |

The majority of books use the dime line; some keep the dime line until the favorite hits –1.95. The dime line THP is listed below.

| 10-CENT THP | DOG PRICE | FAV PRICE | BOOK EARN ON 30K |
|---|---|---|---|
| 2.33% | +1.00 | -1.10 | $697 |
| 2.12% | +1.10 | -1.20 | $635 |
| 1.94% | +1.20 | -1.30 | $581 |
| 1.78% | +1.30 | -1.40 | $533 |
| 1.64% | +1.40 | -1.50 | $491 |
| 1.52% | +1.50 | -1.60 | $454 |

A small minority of sportsbooks still uses the 20-cent line. The THP may be up, but the handle typically is much lower. Bookmaker.com is the best-known book that still uses the 20-cent line; their reputation is such that they don't need the reduced line to attract players. Other books simply would rather not take a whole lot of action on baseball.

| 20-CENT THP | DOG PRICE | FAV PRICE | BOOK EARN ON 30K |
|---|---|---|---|
| 4.35% | +1.00 | -1.20 | $1304 |
| 3.98% | +1.10 | -1.30 | $1192 |
| 3.65% | +1.20 | -1.40 | $1094 |
| 3.36% | +1.30 | -1.50 | $1008 |
| 3.11% | +1.40 | -1.60 | $931 |
| 2.88% | +1.50 | -1.70 | $863 |

### Practical Hold Percentage

Odds will usually move during the day. Sportsbooks don't want to get too lopsided on one side, and adjust the line in order to balance out the action. So what moves the line?

One reason for the line move might be self-preservation for a book. If other sportsbooks are moving the line one way, the sports book might move the line on "air" and follow suit without taking bets that would move the number by themselves. Books want even action, and slow moving lines certainly don't create that.

Another reason might be a lineup change or development that wasn't known in the original number. A player like Mike Trout can be worth twenty-five cents on the line. If he is out of the lineup, you'll see the odds on Anaheim move quickly to reflect his absence.

However, the main reason a sports book will move the line is just plain old cash. If the current line is creating one-way action, the book gives the unpopular team a more attractive price.

THP is what a book expects to hold; Practical Hold Percentage is what the book actually holds. In 2014, Nevada's 187 sportsbooks won $227.04 million on $3.9 billion bet (both the highest in history). The PHP: 5.8%. Booking bets to the masses can be quite profitable.

# THE IMPACT OF REDUCED JUICE ON A BETTOR

We have determined the impact of a 20-cent line on a sportsbook; let's see how it affects the bettor. Assume a 54% bettor is betting into a 20-cent line. He will risk $100 on 100 games, at the standard -110 juice:

Each win = $90.91 in profit (100 win/110 risk)
Each loss = $100 in loss
100 * 100 = $10,000 total risked

Win 54 games: 54 * $90.91 = $4,909 win
Lose 46 games: 46 * 100 = $4,600 loss

$4,909 - $4,600 = $309 profit

**$309 profit divided by $10,000 risked=**
**3.1% return on investment**

If you have a reduced juice book:

Win 54 games: 54 * 95.23 = $5,143 win
Lose 46 games: 46 * 100 = $4,600 loss

**$5143 – $4600 = $542 in profits=**
**5.4% return on investment**

Having access to a reduced juice book will give a $100 bettor an additional $233 in profits after one hundred bets.

# WHERE TO BET IN LAS VEGAS

Twenty years ago, there were about 40 different sportsbooks in Las Vegas offering unique lines and different levels of service to sports bettors. That's not the case anymore; consolidation and streamlining has dropped that number down to 14 unique lines being offered around town.

There are still over seventy sportsbooks in the Las Vegas area. Most of these books deal a dime line on the money line and a 20-cent line on totals. Some of the bigger companies, however, deal a higher line. MGM Resorts gives its bettors a 20-cent line on both the money line and totals. Stations, Caesars, and the Stratosphere deal a 15-cent line on money line bets. That doesn't mean you will never find the best price at one of these sportsbooks, but it does make it less likely.

Like the casinos housing these sportsbooks, no two are alike. Some exude class and sophistication. Some are smoke-filled old school casinos filled with loud, opinionated gamblers ranting about a horse that stumbled out of the gate. Some have unique lines, while others have sports apps that let you stay in your seat while betting with your phone. There is a flavor for all tastes out there. Here are a few of the best places to watch a game in Vegas:

**The Westgate Superbook** set the standard for others to follow, and arguably is the most famous brick and mortar sportsbook in the world. It is huge with a ton of TVs, although does need to do some updating if it wants to stay up there with the Venetians and Mirages of the sports betting world. Located just east of the strip, the Superbook is one of the few remaining independent sportsbooks in town. It isn't fancy with a lot of bells and whistles, but a great place to watch and bet a game. No app.

The **MGM Grand Sportsbook** renovated their sportsbook a few years ago and it still looks new and clean. There is a lot of action here; the sportsbook hosts so many sporting events (boxing, basketball, UFC) that it is typically crowded and full of energy. There are plenty of big leather chairs and big TV screens to watch the games. No App. Huge vig for baseball.

**Mandalay Bay** is a favorite of many old timers who remember when it opened in the 1990s. Sadly, the TVs could be the same. While it is still a great sportsbook to take in a game, it could use some updating. Part of the MGM family, the sportsbook doesn't have an app and deals a high vig.

**Lagasse's Stadium is** more than a sportsbook. It is also a bar, a restaurant, a casino and a lounge. Waitresses are plentiful, but you'll have to buy a certain amount of food and drink to get a seat during busy times. That shouldn't be a problem if you are hanging out all day with friends watching some baseball. The only other downside to Lagasse's Stadium is that the main seating area TV screens are showing their age and could use updating. Regardless, Lagasse's Stadium is one of the best sportsbook in Las Vegas. Just don't expect to get a bargain. No app.

**Caesars Sportsbook** is a must-see for the sports betting fan. It had been showing its age in the past, but the sportsbook has made some nice updates adding nearly all HD big screens and made other small improvements in recent years. Seating is very comfortable but cocktail service is a little slow and is rarely comped. No app.

**Cosmopolitan Race and Sports Book** is located on the second floor of the Marquee Nightclub. A CG Technology book, it may be on the smaller side but still is a great place to watch a game. Like other CTG books, the place is smoke free with an app that makes placing a bet very easy.

**The Bellagio Sportsbook** was one of the last of the Vegas sportsbooks to comp drinks; that is no longer the case however. Even so, the sportsbook is a great place to spend a day watching baseball. Drink tickets aren't hard to get, especially with a friendly tip to the hard-working sportsbook writer. There a place to get low-priced bar food nearby, and the poker room is close as well. No app.

**Wynn Sportsbook**: seats are at a definite premium during busy sports days. That usually shouldn't be a concern during baseball season. If you stay at the hotel, you'll be able to get a seat in any case. Drink tickets are pricey; if you aren't betting $200 a game, then prepare to pay for your drinks. It could use an update.

**Aria Sportsbook**: One of the newer sportsbooks in Las Vegas, the Aria has two monster TVs that dominate the sportsbook. Seating is hard to get when there's an NFL game going on, but that isn't the case during baseball season.

**The Venetian sportsbook** underwent a large renovation in 2011 and you can definitely see where the book spent the money. The lighting and TV screens at The Venetian sportsbook are as good as it gets. The place is massive. Seating is extremely comfortable, with great back support, and the cup holder is definitely convenient. There's a separate section for horse bettors, allowing plenty of space for everyone regardless of their favorite sport

**The Mirage sportsbook** underwent a needed major renovation in 2013, taking out a third of the old desk seating and replaced it with big comfortable chairs. They also added a gigantic TV screen that spans almost the entire huge sportsbook.

**The Golden Nugget sportsbook** is one of the last independently operated sportsbooks, good news for line shoppers. This isn't the largest sportsbook in Las Vegas but it's one of the best options for betting in Downtown Vegas. Space is at a premium in downtown casinos, so the sportsbook doesn't have a lot of seating or room when compared to strip properties.

**The Palms** has, in my opinion, the best sportsbook in Las Vegas. It has massive, top-quality, movie sized TV screens, along with a dozen or so other big TVs that make it possible to focus on any game being televised. The only downside is no cocktail service; however, the full service bar is nearby, quick, with a great view of the sportsbook. It doesn't have an app and is run by CTG.

Running a sportsbook can be a headache for a casino. The cost of a quality in-house linesmaker and support staff is high, and the risks are high as well. A sportsbook isn't like a slot machine; it can lose a lot of money for a casino if it is poorly managed. As a result, many casinos are choosing to outsource their sportsbook to companies that will pay rent to the casino and takes the risks (and profits).

In Nevada, the line originators are Boyd Gaming, Caesars, CG Technology, MGM Resorts, South Point Casino, Stations, Stratosphere, William Hill, and Wynn. While franchising sportsbooks does limit the options available to bettors, it does allow these books to offer apps for online betting. South Point, Boyd, CG Technology, and Stations have apps that allow wagering from anywhere inside Nevada.

Some sportsbooks still make their own lines. Treasure Island, Westgate Superbook, Golden Nugget, Aliante, and Jerry's Nugget all offer an independent line.

## EAST LAS VEGAS

| Casino | Line Originator | Lines |
|---|---|---|
| Sam's Town | Coasts Casinos | 10 cent lines |
| Suncoast | Coasts Casinos | 10 cent lines |
| Hard Rock Hotel | CG Technology | 10 cent lines |
| Eastside Cannery | South Point Casino | 10 cent lines |
| Boulder Station | Station Casinos | 15 cent line |
| Santa Fe Station | Station Casinos | 15 cent line |
| Arizona Charlie's Boulder | Stratosphere | 15 cent line |
| Hooter's | William Hill | 10 cent lines |

## DOWNTOWN SPORTSBOOKS

| Casino | Line Originator | Lines |
|---|---|---|
| California | Coasts Casinos | 10 cent lines |
| Fremont | Coasts Casinos | 10 cent lines |
| Harrah's | Caesars Entertainment | 15 cent line |

| Casino | Line Originator | Lines |
|---|---|---|
| The Quad | Caesars Entertainment | 15 cent line |
| Golden Nugget | Independent | 10 cent lines |
| El Cortez | Station Casinos | 15 cent line |
| Binions | William Hill | 10 cent lines |
| The D Las Vegas | William Hill | 10 cent lines |
| Four Queens | William Hill | 10 cent lines |
| Golden Gate | William Hill | 10 cent lines |
| Plaza | William Hill | 10 cent lines |

## SOUTH OF STRIP

| Casino | Line Originator | Lines |
|---|---|---|
| M Resort | CG Technology | 10 cent lines |
| Silverton | CG Technology | 10 cent lines |
| South Point Casino | South Point Casino | 10 cent lines |

## WEST OF STRIP

| Casino | Line Originator | Lines |
|---|---|---|
| Gold Coast | Coasts Casinos | 10 cent lines |
| Orleans | Coasts Casinos | 10 cent lines |
| Rio | Caesars Entertainment | 15 cent line |
| Palms | CG Technology | 10 cent lines |
| Palace Station | Station Casinos | 15 cent line |
| Wild Wild West | Station Casinos | 15 cent line |

## NORTH SPORTSBOOKS

| Casino | Line Originator | Lines |
|---|---|---|
| Rampart | South Point Casino | 10 cent lines |
| Red Rock | Station Casinos | 15 cent line |
| Arizona Charlie's Decatur | Stratosphere | 15 cent line |
| Aliante | Independent | 5 cent lines |

# STRIP SPORTSBOOKS

| Casino | Line Originator | Lines |
|---|---|---|
| Bally's | Caesars Entertainment | 15 cent line |
| Caesars Palace | Caesars Entertainment | 15 cent line |
| Flamingo | Caesars Entertainment | 15 cent line |
| Paris | Caesars Entertainment | 15 cent line |
| Planet Hollywood | Caesars Entertainment | 15 cent line |
| Cosmopolitan | CG Technology | 10 cent lines |
| Hard Rock Hotel | CG Technology | 10 cent lines |
| Palazzo | CG Technology | 10 cent lines |
| Tropicana | CG Technology | 10 cent lines |
| Venetian | CG Technology | 10 cent lines |
| Treasure Island | Independent | 10 cent lines |
| Westgate LV Superbook | Independent | 10 cent lines |
| Circus Circus | MGM Resorts | 20 cent lines |
| Aria | MGM Resorts | 20 cent lines |
| Bellagio | MGM Resorts | 20 cent lines |
| Excalibur | MGM Resorts | 20 cent lines |
| Luxor | MGM Resorts | 20 cent lines |
| Mandalay Bay | MGM Resorts | 20 cent lines |
| MGM Grand | MGM Resorts | 20 cent lines |
| Mirage | MGM Resorts | 20 cent lines |
| Monte Carlo | MGM Resorts | 20 cent lines |
| New York New York | MGM Resorts | 20 cent lines |
| Stratosphere | Stratosphere | 15 cent line |
| Ellis Island | William Hill | 10 cent lines |
| Hooter's | William Hill | 10 cent lines |
| Riviera | William Hill | 10 cent lines |
| Silver Sevens | William Hill | 10 cent lines |
| SLS | William Hill | 10 cent lines |
| Tuscany | William Hill | 10 cent lines |
| Encore | Wynn Resorts | 10 cent lines |
| Wynn Las Vegas | Wynn Resorts | 10 cent lines |

# THE MONEY LINE

The most common way to bet baseball is using the money line. The money line is simply the odds on which team will win the game. In this way, baseball is different from football and basketball in the betting world. While bookmakers can use point spreads to even things out between two basketball teams, the low number of runs in a baseball game usually eliminates that possibility. This simplifies things for most bettors. Just pick the winner, and you win the money.

Knowing how to read the money line is important, however. A bettor who consistently risks $180 to win $100 has to win over 64% of his wagers simply to break even. The underdog backer, betting $100 to win $170, only has to win 37% of the time to make his money back.

It is that needed win percentage that makes betting on heavy favorites so gruesome. At times, I will risk money on these "sure things". If I believe a team has an 80% chance of winning a game and the odds are -180, I'll close my eyes and pull the trigger. However, I'm not happy about it. It is boring when you win, and execrable when you lose.

To bettors who make their own line and like to translate a team's expected winning percentage into its own true line, the process is simple:

Favorite line:
((1-expected win percentage) / expected win percentage) * -1

If a team has a 60% chance of winning, the formula will look like this:

((1-60%) / 60%) * -1 = -1.50 line.
On underdogs, we reverse the formula and no negative number needed:

40% / (1-40%) = +1.50 true line.

The table below shows the true line on a team depending on its chances of winning the game.

## TRUE LINE/ WIN PERCENTAGE TABLE

| WIN % | TRUE LINE | WIN % | T LINE | WIN % | T LINE |
|-------|-----------|-------|--------|-------|--------|
| 25% | $3.00 | 45% | $1.22 | 65% | -$1.86 |
| 26% | $2.85 | 46% | $1.17 | 66% | -$1.94 |
| 27% | $2.70 | 47% | $1.13 | 67% | -$2.03 |
| 28% | $2.57 | 48% | $1.08 | 68% | -$2.13 |
| 29% | $2.45 | 49% | $1.04 | 69% | -$2.23 |
| 30% | $2.33 | 50% | $1.00 | 70% | -$2.33 |
| 31% | $2.23 | 51% | -$1.04 | 71% | -$2.45 |
| 32% | $2.13 | 52% | -$1.08 | 72% | -$2.57 |
| 33% | $2.03 | 53% | -$1.13 | 73% | -$2.70 |
| 34% | $1.94 | 54% | -$1.17 | 74% | -$2.85 |
| 35% | $1.86 | 55% | -$1.22 | 75% | -$3.00 |
| 36% | $1.78 | 56% | -$1.27 | 76% | -$3.17 |
| 37% | $1.70 | 57% | -$1.33 | 77% | -$3.35 |
| 38% | $1.63 | 58% | -$1.38 | 78% | -$3.55 |
| 39% | $1.56 | 59% | -$1.44 | 79% | -$3.76 |
| 40% | $1.50 | 60% | -$1.50 | 80% | -$4.00 |
| 41% | $1.44 | 61% | -$1.56 | 81% | -$4.26 |
| 42% | $1.38 | 62% | -$1.63 | 82% | -$4.56 |
| 43% | $1.33 | 63% | -$1.70 | 83% | -$4.88 |
| 44% | $1.27 | 64% | -$1.78 | 84% | -$5.25 |

# DECIMAL ODDS

European sportsbooks use decimal odds rather than the "American" type of line. Decimal odds count the initial wager, plus what the bettor would get back after he won. A -110 favorite is listed as a 1.91 favorite ($1 bet, plus 91 cents winnings). A +120 favorite (money line odds) is 2.20 ($1 bet, plus $1.20 winnings). Decimal odds are easier to work with if you know how to calculate the conversion:

For underdog conversions to decimal odds: 1+ money line
For favorite conversions: 1 - (1/money line)

For decimal odds of 2.00 or higher: money line = (decimal - 1) *100
For decimal odds less than 2.00: money line = (-100)/ (decimal -1)

| Money Line | Decimal | exp Win% | ROI |
|:---:|:---:|:---:|:---:|
| -900 | 1.11 | 90% | 11% |
| -300 | 1.33 | 75% | 33.3% |
| -200 | 1.50 | 67% | 50% |
| Pick | 2.00 | 50% | 100% |
| +200 | 3.00 | 33% | 200% |
| +300 | 4.00 | 25% | 300% |
| +900 | 10.00 | 10% | 900% |

To convert decimal odds to an expected winning percentage, simply divide 1 by the odds. For example, the Royals are listed as favorites with odds of 1.65:

$$1 / 1.65 = .606$$

Kansas City's odds of winning, plus the book's vig, is 60.6%.

# FRACTIONAL ODDS

Fractional odds are popular in horseracing as well as in United Kingdom and Ireland. They're also known as British odds. They are represented as fractions (6/4, 2/1, 1/3) and indicate the net payout earned relative to the amount staked. Different from the decimal format, they show the possible profit (the amount of bet is excluded). Odds of 2/1 (the way to say it is "two to one", or less commonly "two to one against") imply that the bettor would have $200 profit on a $100 bet. If the odd is 1/2 ("one to two", or "two to one on"), the bettor would have $50 profit on a $100 bet. Odds of 1/1 are also known as evens or even money.

Converting this format into decimal odds is very easy; just divide the fractions and add 1. (3/2+1=2.50)

**Hong Kong odds** are starting to come into play with the development of powerful Asian sportsbooks. HK odds are just like fractional format, except they're expressed in decimals. To convert it in decimal format just add 1 (0.50 is 1/2 in fractions and 1.50 in decimals).

# THE RUN LINE

The Run Line is a point spread married to a money line. Instead of betting that a team will win the game on the money line, you instead bet with a run line of 1.5. A favorite is listed at -1.5; they would need to win by at least two runs to win the bet. An underdog is listed at +1.5; a one run loss or straight up win for the underdog would win the bet. A bettor can trade a run for extra dollar value on the bet, or buy a run for an extra price.

Historically, a single run wins about 27.7% of all games. This number, however, has to be separated into home games and road games. Road teams are more likely to win by more than one run because they will get nine chances to score in a game. If the road team is winning by one run in the ninth inning, they keep hitting and can keep scoring runs. The table below lists the margin of victory for road teams. On average, the road team wins by one run 25% of the time. A road team favorite will cover the -1.5 runs 75% of the time that road team wins the game.

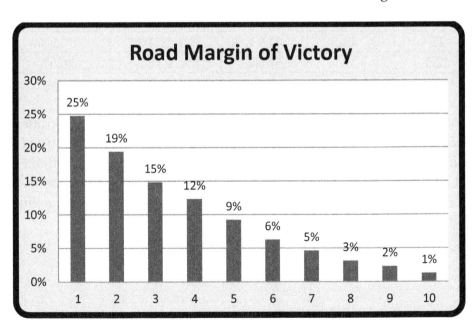

The 75% win rate needs to be adjusted depending on the Over/Under line, however. If more runs are expected in a game, then it will be less likely the game will result in a one-run victory for either team. The table below shows six years of data for road teams. When the total is seven runs, a road team will win by one run almost 29% of the time. When the total is 10.5, they'll win by one run just 21% of the time.

**ROAD TEAM**

| Total | Games | Rd Wins | | 1 Run Rd | >1 Road Win |
|-------|-------|---------|---|----------|-------------|
| 6.5 | 721 | 45.9% | | 26.6% | 73.4% |
| 7 | 2015 | 44.2% | | 28.9% | 71.1% |
| 7.5 | 3286 | 46.1% | | 28.5% | 71.5% |
| 8 | 3620 | 46.5% | | 25.0% | 75.0% |
| 8.5 | 4987 | 46.2% | | 23.7% | 76.3% |
| 9 | 5032 | 46.0% | | 24.0% | 76.0% |
| 9.5 | 3712 | 45.3% | | 23.5% | 76.5% |
| 10 | 1825 | 45.4% | | 22.0% | 78.0% |
| 10.5 | 1067 | 44.9% | | 21.3% | 78.7% |
| 11 | 343 | 42.6% | | 21.2% | 78.8% |
| 11.5 | 123 | 51.2% | | 22.2% | 77.8% |
| 12 | 48 | 47.9% | | 26.1% | 73.9% |
| 12.5 | 31 | 54.8% | | 23.5% | 76.5% |

Betting home teams on the run line is a dangerous proposition. Road teams always get nine at bats, even if they are winning. Not true for home teams. When you bet a home team on the run line, you will likely get only eight at bats to win by two. There are exceptions; a two run walk off home in the ninth is always fun when you bet the home team run line. However, those situations are rare.

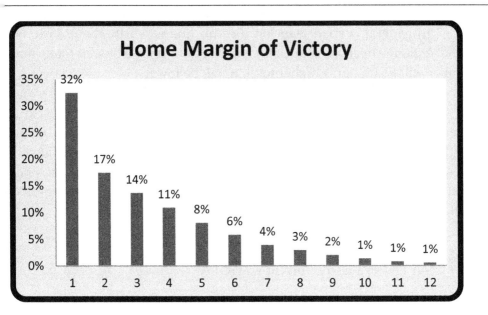

Over the last eight years, 31.5% of all home wins have been by one run. Like the road team however, that number varies depending on what the total is for the game. The lower the number, the more likely a home team will win by one run. When the total is seven runs, a home team will win by one run 38.3% of the time. When it is 11 runs, a home team historically has won by one run 29% of the time.

| Total | Games | Hm Wins | 1 Run HW | >1 Home Wins |
|---|---|---|---|---|
| 6.5 | 721 | 54.1% | 36.9% | 63.1% |
| 7 | 2015 | 55.8% | 38.3% | 61.7% |
| 7.5 | 3286 | 53.9% | 34.3% | 65.7% |
| 8 | 3620 | 53.5% | 33.9% | 66.1% |
| 8.5 | 4987 | 53.8% | 32.8% | 67.2% |
| 9 | 5032 | 54.0% | 32.2% | 67.8% |
| 9.5 | 3712 | 54.7% | 29.6% | 70.4% |
| 10 | 1825 | 54.6% | 26.5% | 73.5% |
| 10.5 | 1067 | 55.1% | 28.4% | 71.6% |
| 11 | 343 | 57.4% | 28.9% | 71.1% |

In general, a road team on the run line is worth about 55 to 60 cents. A home team is about 30 cents higher. With a lower total, that number will be higher; a higher total, it will be lower.

Most bettors use run lines to knock down heavy favorites to a decent number. However, the frustration of having the team you bet on win by only one run can take a toll on a bettor. One way to avoid this disaster is to split your bet between the money line and run line. Let's say Boston is a -133 favorite on the road at Oakland. Instead of betting $100 on the Red Sox using the run line, I would bet:

- $55 on Boston to win $41
- $41 on Boston -1.5 runs to win $51

If Boston loses, I'm out $96. If Boston wins by more than one run, I'm up $92. If Boston wins by one run, I break even. By manipulating bets this way, a bettor can get Boston − 1 for -104.

This is my favorite way to bet medium to heavy favorites, assuming the run line is a fair price. I don't pay a lot of extra juice, and I still have my money on the team I want. Breaking even when my team wins by just one run keeps the pain away.

Another option open for bettors is to take an underdog on the plus side of the run line. Instead of giving up 1.5 runs, a gambler would collect if his team won outright or lost by just one run. Few recreational bettors take this play; I dislike it simply because I enjoy collecting the juicy payoffs when an underdog wins the game. It is something I look at on each game, however. The public overwhelmingly takes favorites on the run line, occasionally pushing the value on the other side high enough for me to take a stab at it.

Sportsbooks generally follow these guidelines when it comes to setting a run line price:

| Home | Line | | Away | Run | Line |
|------|------|------|------|-----|------|
| -200 | -1.5 | -105 | -200 | -1.5 | -130 |
| -190 | -1.5 | 100 | -190 | -1.5 | -125 |
| -180 | -1.5 | 105 | -180 | -1.5 | -120 |
| -170 | -1.5 | 110 | -170 | -1.5 | -115 |
| -160 | -1.5 | 120 | -160 | -1.5 | -110 |
| -150 | -1.5 | 130 | -150 | -1.5 | 100 |
| -140 | -1.5 | 140 | -140 | -1.5 | 110 |
| -130 | -1.5 | 150 | -130 | -1.5 | 120 |
| -120 | -1.5 | 160 | -120 | -1.5 | 130 |
| -110 | -1.5 | 170 | -110 | -1.5 | 135 |

One other betting option is the alternate run line. The alternate run line handicaps the dog by 1.5 runs. At one time, taking the alternate run line was lucrative. The lines tightened up, however, and the betting opportunities weren't quite as evident. It is something to keep in mind though. There are still a lot of instances where taking the underdog –1.5 is profitable.

*The most valuable thing you can make is a mistake – you can't learn anything from being perfect.*
*Adam Osborne*

# FINDING AN EDGE

You don't need to be sharp to win a bet. David Threlfall was not a betting man. With no interest in sports or the horses, the first time the science fiction fan placed a wager was to change his life forever.

In 1964, he asked British bookmaker for odds on a man walking on the moon. William Hill made the odds 1000-1. The oddsmaker for William Hill said later, "I reckoned the true odds were more like three to one against but to have offered this would have been absurd. We wouldn't have got any more bets."

News of the bet spread around the world and others put their money down as the odds tumbled. As the space race continued through the 1960s, David was inundated with offers from gamblers offering to buy his betting slip from him for thousands of pounds.

However, he stood firm and so it was that at a precise moment in the summer of 1969, when Neil Armstrong took his giant step for mankind, William Hill's profit margins took a giant leap backwards.

David was at television studios in London to be presented with his check for £10,000 live on ITV's special Man on the Moon as Neil Armstrong stepped onto the moon. David, 26 years old at the time, explained why he had placed the amazing bet.

"In 1963 I heard President Kennedy make a speech in which he said there would be an American on the moon by the end of the decade. I thought if a bookmaker was prepared to offer reasonable odds it would be a common sense bet."

No reason to cry for William Hill, however. The sportsbook also took major action on a Mars landing by 1973 (4 to 1 odds). 45 years later, we are still waiting.

# TOTALS

When you think of "key numbers" in handicapping, football and the number three comes immediately to mind. In baseball totals, those key numbers are seven and nine. A past Chicago-St. Louis game illustrates this fact. Carlos Zambrano and Adam Wainwright were on the mound. Both pitchers struggled in April, and the Over/Under line opened up at 8.5. I waited, however. I liked the Under and was hoping to see the number rise once the betting public looked at the weather forecast (wind blowing out) and considered the recent form of both pitchers.

It is a good thing I did. The bettors loved the Over. Heavy action on the Over pushed the line to nine runs, a significant move. Sportsbooks don't like moving on or off nine runs. The chart below detailing the number of runs scored in each game will give an indication as to why:

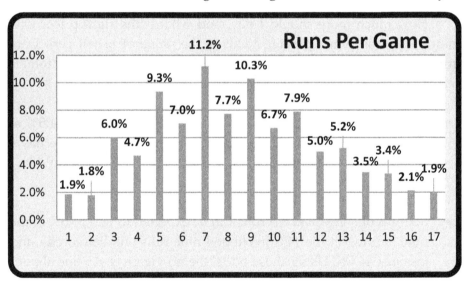

More games land on seven, nine, and 11 runs than any other number. The reason is simple: a tie game requires at least one more run to score before it ends. A game tied at four in the late innings more often than not will end with nine runs scored in the game; just like 3-3 games will usually end with a 4-3 victory from one team.

It is vital to get on the right side of these key numbers. If I like the Over in a game and the overnight total is at 8.5 runs, chances are I will make an immediate play. Waiting until the next day, in the hopes of seeing that total drop to eight runs, is not worth the risk of seeing it rise up to nine. To put it into perspective: 54.9% of all baseball games end up with nine or more runs scored in a game. 55.7% of all baseball games end up with nine or less runs scored per game. By hook or by crook, I pull out all my tricks to get on the right side of nine when betting my totals.

Up to a point, however. Getting on the right side of nine has a price, and if it is too expensive then I'll just take what I can get. As I said earlier, many sportsbooks don't like moving off the key numbers. For this reason, I'll sometimes see one book with a total of nine and another with 9.5. The sportsbooks that don't adjust the total will simply adjust the price: if I want the Under 9.5, I pay a higher price.

How much more should I pay, and what is the right price? One common question when playing totals is the value of a half run. Data from the last three years tells us that games land on nine when the total is nine about 11% of the time. In other words:

- Bettor A playing over nine runs can be expected to win 44.5% of the time, lose 44.5%, and push 11% of the time. Since he has a 50/50 chance at winning, the no-vig Over/Under 9 line should be -100.

- Bettor B playing Over 8.5 runs can be expected to win 55.5% of the time (adding in the 11% likelihood nine runs will be scored), and lose just 44.5%. Using those odds, the no-vig Over 8.5 line should be -124.5.

The half run from 8.5 to nine is worth between 24 and 25 cents. To go from seven runs to 7.5 is worth 27 cents; from eight to 8.5 runs is worth 17 cents.

| Total #1 | Total #2 | Gms Over | Under | Push | Price |
|---|---|---|---|---|---|
| 7 | 7.5 | 1722 | 1822 | 486 | 27 cents |
| 8 | 8.5 | 3236 | 3430 | 576 | 17 cents |
| 9 | 9.5 | 4342 | 4610 | 1112 | 25 cents |
| 10 | 10.5 | 1688 | 1694 | 268 | 16 cents |
| 11 | 11.5 | 268 | 340 | 78 | 29 cents |

The decision to wait on betting the Under in the Chicago-St. Louis paid off as the Cubs beat up on Wainwright and the Cardinals 8-1. Understanding totals, and the key numbers to dance around, will often allow you to `steal' a bet while others on the same side have losing tickets.

## THE RUN SCORING TREND

Run scoring in the MLB peaked in 2000 (10.2 runs per game) and has dropped like a rock since. Baseball is now dominated by elite pitching and defense. In 2004, there were 9.6 runs scored per game. The over/under results were about 50/50, once pushes are tossed from the equation. In 2014, there were 8.3 runs per game, a 1.3 RPG drop from 10 years earlier. There were 1,100 games that went over the total, and 1,217 games that stayed Under. A small difference, but it still shows that the value has leaned towards the Under in recent years. It isn't enough to blindly play Unders, but it should make one dig deeper before playing an Over.

The table below is also a good way to illustrate the dangers of using averages over median. An average is simple: add up all the numbers, then divide by how many numbers there are. In other words, it is the sum divided by the count.

The median is the middle value in an ordered list of numbers. You have to order the numbers from top to bottom, and then find the middle value. This is the reason why the average Total is usually about a half run lower than the average runs per game. There is no limit to how many runs can be scored in the game and go over the total. There is a limit, however, to how few runs can be scored in a game and go under a total.

For example, let's say Arizona is playing a two game series at San Diego. Both games have seven runs as the Total. The first game has a 2-0 final score. The second game ends up 10-8. Using a runs per game average in this instance would not tell a bettor the true story. Not using a median RPG could lead a bettor to mistakenly play too many Overs when betting totals.

| Year | RPG | Total | Over-Under-Push | Over-Under-Push |
|------|-----|-------|-----------------|-----------------|
| 2004 | 9.6 | 9.1 | 1171-1184-107 | 48%-48%-4% |
| 2005 | 9.2 | 8.9 | 1100-1217-137 | 45%-50%-6% |
| 2006 | 9.7 | 9.2 | 1178-1164-113 | 48%-47%-5% |
| 2007 | 9.6 | 9.1 | 1147-1177-130 | 47%-48%-5% |
| 2008 | 9.3 | 8.9 | 1148-1199-109 | 47%-49%-4% |
| 2009 | 9.2 | 8.9 | 1106-1231-110 | 45%-50%-4% |
| 2010 | 8.8 | 8.4 | 1123-1213-122 | 46%-49%-5% |
| 2011 | 8.6 | 8.1 | 1185-1141-134 | 48%-46%-5% |
| 2012 | 8.6 | 8.2 | 1131-1210-120 | 46%-49%-5% |
| 2013 | 8.3 | 8.0 | 1171-1184-107 | 46%-50%-4% |
| 2014 | 8.3 | 7.8 | 1100-1217-137 | 46%-49%-5% |

*Yesterday's home runs don't win today's games. – Babe Ruth*

# FIRST INNING WAGERS

A relatively new bet available for today's baseball bettor is the first inning wager. The first inning baseball bet is an Over/Under bet with a total of .5 runs, with the juice adjusted based on the overall total of the game. Bettors simply bet if they believe a run will be scored in the first inning of a game or not. It is essentially the crack cocaine of the baseball world. You don't wait it out nine innings; you'll know after one inning if you won or lost. This keeps things simple. A bettor doesn't have to worry about the bullpen or the bottom of the order. It is simply the starting pitchers vs. the top half of the opposing team's lineup. Sportsbooks will make the bettor pay for this simplicity, however. Bettors usually bet into a 30-cent line on these first inning wagers. The bet will often look like this:

Will there be a run scored in the first inning?

Yes -115
No -115

Like most major league bets, the starting pitchers are the key factors in the price of this prop bet. Some pitchers have a history of struggling in the first inning before settling down. Others will start out fast, but get hit as they start to tire. Lines typically aren't adjusted for these types of pitchers; a bettor willing to put his work into this prop bet can find some edges.

A team's lineup is important as well. Some old school managers will put a couple of speed guys at the top of the lineup, despite the fact that these players don't get on base as well as some slower hitters in the lineup. These are good teams to bet the "No". Other teams, like Milwaukee and the Angels, stack their best hitters at the top of the lineup. One should look to bet "Yes" with these type of teams.

Another major factor is the total in the game. The more runs expected, the higher the "No" odds will be. The table below details how often at least one run is scored in the first inning.

| Games | Total | Yes | No |
|---|---|---|---|
| 343 | 11 | 60% | 40% |
| 1067 | 10.5 | 61% | 39% |
| 1825 | 10 | 56% | 44% |
| 3712 | 9.5 | 55% | 45% |
| 5032 | 9 | 53% | 47% |
| 4987 | 8.5 | 52% | 48% |
| 3621 | 8 | 49% | 51% |
| 3286 | 7.5 | 48% | 52% |
| 2015 | 7 | 47% | 53% |
| 721 | 6.5 | 40% | 60% |

Betting into a 30-cent line makes things tough for a first inning bettor, but one can still find an occasional bet. The limits are low on these types of bets, meaning a sportsbook won't take a lot of money before they move the line. One will often find big differences in prices between books, so shop carefully.

*If what you are doing is not moving you towards your goals, then it's moving you away from your goals. – Brian Tracy*

# FIFTH INNING WAGERS

It was all over for the upstart Royals in the 2014 Wild Card game against the A's. Kansas City was down 7-3 heading into the bottom of the eighth. Oakland ace Jon Lester still going strong, having thrown just 94 pitches. The only question was whether Lester could finish the game himself or leave it to the bullpen in the ninth.

A seeing-eye single that just got over Lester's head and past the shortstop was of little concern to A's backers. Neither was the subsequent Alcides Escobar stolen base. People were asking why the Royals were stealing down four runs with only six outs left, but that was just one more reason to mock Royals manager Ned Yost.

A Nori Aoki ground out left Kansas City with just five outs, still needing four runs. Lorenzo Cain, however, continued the rally with an RBI single. It was now a 7-4 game. Cain, knowing Lester shows no interest in baserunners, stole second. Eric Hosmer walked. Lester was pulled. Billy Butler singled in a run. Pinch runner Terrance Gore stole second. A wild pitch scored Hosmer and advanced Gore. Alex Gordon walks, then stole second. It was now 7-6 with runners on second and third and still only one out.

The rally ended there. Strikeouts to Salvador Perez and Omar Infante left Oakland clinging to a one-run lead. It wasn't enough, however. A single, sacrifice, stolen base, and sacrifice fly tied it up for Kansas City in the bottom of the ninth to push the game into extra innings. There it remained scoreless until the twelfth, when the A's scored a run on a RBI single by Alberto Callapso to take a one-run lead.

The Royals rallied again. Perez made up for his eighth inning failure with a game winning line drive that just got under third baseman Josh Donaldson's glove. Kansas City had pulled it out. A's fans were stunned. Handicappers who bet on the A's were pissed. A near certain victory had been lost thanks to a series of fortunate bounces and good timing.

Nothing is more frustrating than losing a late lead because of a shaky bullpen, a broken bat single, or a blown call by the umpire. Blowing four-run leads aren't common, but they happen. When they do, more than just a bettor's bankroll is damaged. The psychological effects of losing a game once thought to have been in the bag can carry over far beyond just that night's game.

One way to combat this is the use of fifth inning bets. Fifth inning bets are wagers on which team will be leading after five innings. A bettor worried about a team's bullpen can take the pen entirely out of the equation by making these fifth inning bets. He could bet a half unit on the fifth inning and a half unit on the game. A blown save, while still painful, is easier to take if you have already won your fifth inning wager.

At least that is the theory. The question remains: how often will these bets actually cut a handicapper's losses? Using five years' worth of data and ignoring fifth inning ties, we can determine how such a strategy works:

|  | Fifth Inning Wins | Game |
|---|---|---|
| Road | 46.5% | 46.2% |
| Home | 53.5% | 53.8% |

A bettor splitting his wagers on the fifth inning and the complete game would show a slight improvement for road teams while costing him a few bets on home teams. 15% of the games will be tied after five innings; those games are refunded to the bettor.

One problem with this approach is the inability to shop for the best lines. Most books, other than the three mentioned above, will charge 10% juice on these type of bets. The lack of line variety means a handicapper is stuck with whatever line is dealt, unlike complete game wagers.

The data can be broken down a little more:

| | |
|---|---|
| Road wins both fifth and game | 37.2% |
| Road wins fifth, home wins game | 9.3% |
| Home wins both fifth and game | 44.8% |
| Home wins fifth, road wins game | 8.7% |

18% of all games have the team losing after five innings come back to win the game. The chart above shows that road teams will blow a few more games than home teams, but the difference is small (about 10-12 games each season).

So what teams are more likely to blow fifth inning leads? In 2014, the Astros led baseball with 19 blown fifth inning leads. The Yankees were second with 18. This counting statistic, like most counting stats in baseball, doesn't tell the whole story. A good team will have more fifth inning leads and will obviously have more chances to blow those leads. To account for this, we need to use the "Blow Rate". The Blow Rate is the ratio of blown fifth inning leads to overall wins. That is the number a handicapper should focus on if he wants to make fifth inning bets based on what team is most likely to blow a lead.

The Arizona Diamondbacks took the Blow Rate crown for 2014. Arizona had the fifth inning lead 54 times last year. They won only 39 of those games, good for a 38% Blow Rate. The league average Blow Rate was 20% in 2014. The Orioles had the lowest rate in baseball. Their Blow Rate was an incredible 7%. That was the third lowest Blow Rate since 2004; only the Yankees in 2008 (66-3) and 2009 (73-5) were better.

# 2014 Blow Rates

| Team | Win | Loss | Blow Rate | ERA | Rank |
|---|---|---|---|---|---|
| Diamondbacks | 39 | 15 | 38% | 3.92 | 23 |
| Astros | 51 | 19 | 37% | 4.80 | 30 |
| White Sox | 46 | 15 | 33% | 4.38 | 28 |
| Phillies | 49 | 15 | 31% | 3.64 | 18 |
| Rockies | 47 | 13 | 28% | 4.79 | 29 |
| Mets | 58 | 16 | 28% | 3.14 | 8 |
| Yankees | 66 | 18 | 27% | 3.70 | 19 |
| Rangers | 41 | 11 | 27% | 4.02 | 24 |
| Reds | 54 | 13 | 24% | 4.11 | 26 |
| Twins | 46 | 10 | 22% | 3.73 | 21 |
| Pirates | 60 | 13 | 22% | 3.28 | 9 |
| Cardinals | 65 | 13 | 20% | 3.62 | 16 |
| Cubs | 55 | 11 | 20% | 3.61 | 15 |
| Brewers | 61 | 12 | 20% | 3.62 | 16 |
| Marlins | 47 | 9 | 19% | 3.33 | 12 |
| Tigers | 68 | 13 | 19% | 4.29 | 27 |
| Mariners | 63 | 11 | 17% | 2.60 | 1 |
| Athletics | 63 | 11 | 17% | 2.91 | 3 |
| Rays | 54 | 9 | 17% | 3.71 | 20 |
| Red Sox | 48 | 8 | 17% | 3.33 | 12 |
| Angels | 71 | 11 | 15% | 3.52 | 14 |
| Blue Jays | 60 | 9 | 15% | 4.09 | 25 |
| Braves | 61 | 9 | 15% | 3.31 | 11 |
| Giants | 68 | 9 | 13% | 3.01 | 5 |
| Nationals | 70 | 9 | 13% | 3.00 | 4 |
| Royals | 71 | 9 | 13% | 3.30 | 10 |
| Indians | 54 | 6 | 11% | 3.12 | 7 |
| Padres | 54 | 6 | 11% | 2.73 | 2 |
| Dodgers | 73 | 8 | 11% | 3.80 | 22 |
| Orioles | 68 | 5 | 7% | 3.10 | 6 |

# BETTING PARLAYS

Parlays equal sucker bets; that is the consensus in gambling circles since the bettor receives payouts at a much lower ratio than the true odds. In point-spread bets like basketball and football that is true. A two-team parlay pays 2.6 to 1 while the true odds are 3 to 1. A three teamer pays 6 to 1 (7 to 1 true odds), while a four-teamer pays 12-1 with true odds being 15-1. That is leaving a lot of money on the table.

That isn't the case in baseball, however. Baseball parlays are calculated differently since it is a money line sport rather than a point spread sports. A book can't pay 2.6-1 on a two-team parlay if the two teams are -200 favorites. The parlay instead is calculated by the odds of the teams used in the parlay.

Here is an example on money line parlays. Let's say the bettor has $100 in his pocket but likes the Yankees, Red Sox, and Rangers. Rather than bet all three individually, he wants to risk more to win more.

The first step is to determine what the multipliers would be for each game. To do this, we divide the total payout (risk + win) by the risk amount:

- Yankees: - 150 to win 100= $250 payout
  250/150 = 1.66

- Red Sox: 100 to win 170= $270 payout
  270/100 = 2.7

- Rangers: 120 to win 100= $220 payout
  220/120 = 1.83

Now that we have the multipliers, we multiply them together to come up with the money line odds of the parlay.

$$1.66 \times 2.7 \times 1.83 = 8.25$$

For every $1 bet, the return is $8.25, including the risk amount. Therefore, the $100 bettor, winning his three-team parlay, will collect $825 from the sportsbook.

The ability to win a lot of money without investing a lot of money is the benefit of betting parlays. The negative is obvious: it is a lot harder to win three games than it is to win one. From a mathematical standpoint, however, there is no real advantage or disadvantage to playing parlays. True payoff odds are used, so there is no leaving money on the table like a football parlay.

*Success is simply a matter of luck. Ask any failure. – Earl Wilson*

*A bad worker blames his tools. – Chinese Proverb*

*The road to success and the road to failure are almost exactly the same. – Colin R. Davis*

# INTERLEAGUE PLAY

It used to be simple in baseball. The National League is the National League, the American League is the American League, and never the twain shall meet. At least until the World Series. That all went out the window in 1997. Bud Selig and his cabal decided the game needed some spice to recover from the strike, and interleague play was it.

In the early years of play, bragging rights were hard to come by. By the end of the 2004 season, the American League had won 959 games while the NL won 988.

The American League has begun asserting its dominance in recent years, however. The AL has won nearly 55% of interleague games since 2004:

| Year | Record | Win % | Profit |
|---|---|---|---|
| 2004 | 131-125 | 51.2% | $140 |
| 2005 | 140-116 | 54.7% | $1,530 |
| 2006 | 155-102 | 60.3% | $4,485 |
| 2007 | 141-115 | 55.1% | $910 |
| 2008 | 150-107 | 58.4% | $2,855 |
| 2009 | 142-116 | 55.0% | $925 |
| 2010 | 135-122 | 52.5% | $193 |
| 2011 | 134-125 | 51.7% | $-757 |
| 2012 | 142-114 | 55.5% | $1,644 |
| 2013 | 158-148 | 51.6% | $-129 |
| 2014 | 166-141 | 54.1% | $1,463 |
| Overall | 1594-1331 | 54.5% | $13,259 |

There are several ways to handicap interleague play. The first method a bettor might use involves focusing on an individual team's past performance against the opposing league. The Tigers, Red Sox, and Angels will usually dominate interleague play while Colorado, Houston, and Philadelphia historically struggle. Some teams might like the change interleague play brings to the game. Others might have difficulty adjusting to unfamiliar players, ballparks and different rules. Or a team might just have bad luck. Anything can happen over 15-20 games and a team's poor record in interleague games might just be a fluke. It is up to a handicapper to decide the reasons.

Another method is to assume the league superiority is league-wide. That is, the worst team in the American League is still better than the worst team in the National League. A handicapper who follows this would typically give AL teams a "bonus" when he is making his lines.

In recent years, the American League has been .20 or .25 runs stronger than the National League. A handicapper would add about 15 cents to his line to account for this difference.

There is another variable added to the handicapping puzzle during interleague games. One must account for the rivalry factors in certain series. The Yankees vs. Mets mean a lot more to the teams and fans than a typical Mets-Nationals series. Pay close attention to bullpen use. Many managers may push their top relievers a little harder in order to grab a win against its rivals.

One added warning to handicappers who might give AL teams the generic bonus on the line: National League teams have historically struggled more on the road against the American League than they have at home. Over the last decade, NL teams win 52% of its home games vs. the AL. However, they win only 38% of its road games during interleague play.

|  | Games | Win % | 2009 | 2010 | 2011 | 2012 | 2013 | 2014 |
|---|---|---|---|---|---|---|---|---|
| AL Home, AL Wins | 472 | 58% | 73 | 70 | 74 | 70 | 91 | 94 |
| AL Home, AL Loses | 347 | 42% | 56 | 52 | 55 | 58 | 62 | 64 |
| AL Win % | 819 | 58% | 57% | 57% | 57% | 55% | 60% | 59% |
| NL Home, NL wins | 414 | 50% | 60 | 70 | 70 | 56 | 86 | 72 |
| NL Home, NL loses | 407 | 50% | 69 | 58 | 60 | 72 | 67 | 81 |
| NL Win % | 821 | 50% | 47% | 55% | 54% | 44% | 56% | 47% |

Some bettors love betting interleague games. They believe the added variables mean the lines are softer, and hence, more beatable. Others stay far away, unable to get a "feel" for the games and not willing to bet. I like it because shakes things up. However, adjustments need to be made in order to have success.

**Good Interleague Teams:**
Baltimore, Boston, Detroit, LAA Angels, Yankees

**Poor Interleague Teams:**
Cubs, Cincinnati, Colorado, Houston, Philadelphia

# Team Interleague Winning Percentage

| Team | 2009 | 2010 | 2011 | 2012 | 2013 | 2014 | Last 6 |
|---|---|---|---|---|---|---|---|
| Arizona | 33% | 40% | 56% | 60% | 55% | 35% | 46% |
| Atlanta | 47% | 60% | 67% | 44% | 55% | 35% | 51% |
| Baltimore | 61% | 39% | 39% | 61% | 55% | 60% | 53% |
| Boston | 61% | 72% | 56% | 61% | 69% | 45% | 61% |
| Chicago Cubs | 40% | 44% | 33% | 33% | 65% | 45% | 44% |
| Chicago White Sox | 67% | 83% | 61% | 50% | 40% | 55% | 59% |
| Cincinnati | 40% | 53% | 33% | 47% | 55% | 30% | 43% |
| Cleveland | 28% | 28% | 61% | 44% | 55% | 50% | 44% |
| Colorado | 73% | 60% | 53% | 13% | 25% | 35% | 43% |
| Detroit | 56% | 61% | 39% | 50% | 60% | 60% | 54% |
| Houston | 40% | 20% | 27% | 40% | 40% | 25% | 32% |
| Kansas City | 44% | 44% | 28% | 44% | 45% | 67% | 45% |
| LA Angels | 78% | 61% | 72% | 67% | 50% | 60% | 65% |
| LA Dodgers | 50% | 27% | 40% | 40% | 60% | 55% | 45% |
| Miami | 56% | 47% | 44% | 28% | 45% | 65% | 47% |
| Milwaukee | 33% | 60% | 40% | 40% | 30% | 55% | 43% |
| Minnesota | 67% | 44% | 44% | 50% | 40% | 45% | 48% |
| New York Mets | 33% | 72% | 50% | 53% | 55% | 55% | 53% |
| New York Yankees | 58% | 61% | 72% | 72% | 45% | 65% | 62% |
| Oakland | 28% | 44% | 44% | 56% | 65% | 65% | 50% |
| Philadelphia | 33% | 56% | 60% | 33% | 35% | 35% | 42% |
| Pittsburgh | 53% | 13% | 53% | 56% | 75% | 55% | 51% |
| San Diego | 33% | 60% | 40% | 53% | 40% | 45% | 45% |
| San Francisco | 60% | 55% | 67% | 58% | 30% | 52% | 54% |
| Seattle | 61% | 50% | 50% | 44% | 40% | 45% | 48% |
| St. Louis | 60% | 60% | 55% | 53% | 46% | 40% | 52% |
| Tampa Bay | 72% | 39% | 67% | 50% | 60% | 50% | 56% |
| Texas | 50% | 65% | 48% | 78% | 50% | 50% | 57% |
| Toronto | 39% | 39% | 44% | 50% | 55% | 65% | 49% |
| Washington | 39% | 28% | 53% | 56% | 55% | 50% | 47% |

# BETTING ON STREAKS

Evolution has primed our brains to look for patterns. One apple on the ground means other apples are probably nearby. Distribution of food in the wild is not random; it occurs in clusters. To early man, this knowledge kept them alive. To gamblers, this can lead to some unintended consequences. Seeing patterns where none exists is not good.

One hears all sorts of gambling theories if you hang around a sportsbook long enough. From "always back the Dominican pitcher on a hot day" to "that guy can't pitch in day games because he's a drunk and hung over all the time." Streak bettors aren't quite as nonsensical. However, they do hunt for patterns where none may exist; these gamblers often refuse to bet a team because their opponent is on a winning streak.

Streak bettors operate under a simple theory. Baseball is a game of streaks. Find a team that is on a roll, pound that team while it is hot, and abandon ship once that streak ends. You only lose once using this method. However, is it profitable?

It hasn't been recently. The table below shows how well teams on winnings streaks have done since 2010:

| Streak | Wins | Loss | Profit |
|--------|------|------|--------|
| 3 | 637 | 590 | -1718 |
| 4 | 316 | 321 | -4860 |
| 5 | 159 | 157 | -3442 |
| 6 | 81 | 78 | -591 |
| 7 | 48 | 33 | 837 |
| 8 | 27 | 21 | 51 |
| 9 | 13 | 14 | -324 |
| 10 | 5 | 8 | -560 |
| 11 | 4 | 1 | 310 |
| 12 | 1 | 3 | -200 |
| Total | 4993 | 4828 | -28337 |

A $100 bettor would have lost $28,337 betting on those hot teams. Since only teams on a seven game win streak showed a decent profit, you can safely consider a simple streak system to be a failure.

## HOME TEAMS

We can break it down into more subsets, however. How well do home teams do when they are on a winning streak? It isn't pretty. A gambler would have lost $9,565 betting on teams with a winning streak.

| Streak | Wins | Loss | Profit |
|--------|------|------|--------|
| 3 | 354 | 311 | -5550 |
| 4 | 168 | 151 | -2130 |
| 5 | 79 | 74 | 615 |
| 6 | 45 | 33 | -575 |
| 7 | 23 | 17 | -860 |
| 8 | 14 | 9 | -655 |
| 9 | 5 | 9 | -270 |
| 10 | 1 | 6 | -140 |
| Total | 689 | 610 | -9565 |

## HOME FAVORITES

Do home favorites show a profit? Not at all. Our mythical $100 bettor would have lost almost $9,000 had he blindly bet home favorites.

| Streak | Wins | Loss | Profit |
|--------|------|------|--------|
| 3 | 283 | 231 | -4507 |
| 4 | 148 | 115 | -1981 |
| 5 | 70 | 62 | -2765 |
| 6 | 42 | 22 | 961 |
| 7 | 20 | 16 | -356 |
| 8 | 13 | 6 | 230 |
| 9 | 4 | 7 | -550 |
| Total | 580 | 459 | -8968 |

# HOME DOGS

Home dogs got smashed as well. A bettor would show a $1,520 loss betting on streaking home underdogs.

| Streak | Wins | Loss | Profit |
|--------|------|------|--------|
| 3 | 71 | 77 | 595 |
| 4 | 20 | 36 | -1237 |
| 5 | 9 | 12 | -112 |
| 6 | 3 | 11 | -775 |
| Total | 103 | 136 | -1529 |

# ROAD TEAMS

Road teams showed a little promise. Blindly betting a streaking road team would yield $708 in profits for a $100 bettor, after putting in over $12,000 in action.

| Streak | Wins | Loss | Profit |
|--------|------|------|--------|
| 3 | 285 | 279 | 2194 |
| 4 | 148 | 170 | -1642 |
| 5 | 80 | 83 | -565 |
| 6 | 36 | 45 | -777 |
| 7 | 25 | 15 | 955 |
| 8 | 13 | 12 | 17 |
| 9 | 8 | 5 | 321 |
| 10 | 4 | 2 | 205 |
| Total | 599 | 611 | 708 |

# ROAD FAVORITES

The road team profit angle wasn't because of road favorites, however. Road favorites were down $591.

| Streak | Wins | Loss | Profit |
|--------|------|------|--------|
| 3 | 144 | 107 | 833 |
| 4 | 69 | 71 | -2411 |
| 5 | 47 | 39 | -413 |
| 6 | 20 | 16 | 81 |
| 7 | 16 | 9 | 395 |
| 8 | 11 | 5 | 455 |
| Total | 315 | 250 | -591 |

# ROAD UNDERDOGS

Which leaves us road underdogs. Road dogs showed a nice $1,289 in profits over 642 plays. What does that mean? Most likely nothing…this is data mining at work.

| Streak | Wins | Loss | Profit |
|--------|------|------|--------|
| 3 | 141 | 172 | 1361 |
| 4 | 78 | 99 | 769 |
| 5 | 33 | 44 | -152 |
| 6 | 16 | 29 | -858 |
| 7 | 9 | 6 | 560 |
| Total | 282 | 360 | 1289 |

Summing up the data: Betting on streaking home favorites, home underdogs, and away favorites is a disaster. Road underdogs show a profit but that profit is mostly due to random chance. When playing on streaking teams, make sure you are betting the team for reasons other than the streak itself. Streaks mean nothing by themselves. Momentum is nice to have, but baseball is often like craps. What happened yesterday has little bearing on what happens today.

# THE SHOESHINE BOY

Joe Kennedy, the father of JFK and one of the richest men in America, liked to tell the story of the Shoeshine Boy. "The kid who shined my shoes didn't know me," he said. "He wasn't looking for a tip on the market or anything like that. He was just average and, like everyone else, he was playing the market. All the time he was snapping the polishing cloth over my shoes, he kept telling me what was going to happen that day, what stocks would rise and what the market would do.

"I just listened to him, and when I left the place I thought, 'When the time comes that a shoeshine boy knows as much as I do about what is going on in the stock market, tells me so, and is entirely correct, there's something wrong with either me or the market, and it's time for me to get out.'"

Joe Kennedy sold his stocks and moved his money into real estate, avoiding the crash that wiped out millions of investors. In 1929, his fortune was estimated to be $4 million. Six years later, he was worth $180 million.

The Shoeshine Boy is the standard go-to metaphor for getting out of the stock market. The story most likely isn't 100% true; Wall Street was full of those types of stories at that time. However, the overriding fact holds true: when a shoeshine boy, or bartender, or dude sitting next to you at the bar, starts giving advice on how to get rich, it's time to bail.

The same goes with sports betting. When the Shoeshine Boys are all on one side, the other side is usually the correct place to be. This isn't a new idea. One often hears recreational gamblers describe their betting philosophy as "I pick the side I think is a lock, then bet the other side."

The internet has made it easy to find out what the Shoeshine Boys are thinking. Twitter, ESPN, talk radio all are good barometers of public thinking. Another method has developed in recent years. "Reverse Line Movement" is one of the new buzzwords in sports betting. Line services like SportsOptions are now releasing numbers as to what percentage of bettors are taking a certain side. Subscribers to SportsOptions will know if 90% of the bets are on the Yankees in a particular day; the sportsbooks have given SportsOptions that information.

They don't, however, tell you the amount of money on each side. While the Yankees might get 90% of the bets, we don't know if they are getting 90% of the money. Nine bettors might be betting $10 a game on the Yankees. One bettor could be betting $3,000 on New York's opponent. A bettor might look at the raw bet percentage and think he knows whom the Shoeshine Boys are playing. And he would be right; a team getting 90% of the bets obviously has a lot of the public backing them. However, what if that big bettor is part of the 90% as well?

That's where the reverse line movement comes into play. When 90% of the bets are on one side, the betting line should move higher for that one side. The Yankees may have opened -110, but that line will go to -120 or -130 when everyone is betting New York. When the line doesn't climb, and instead moves the Yankees to +100, red flags need to fly. Reverse line movement is in play. The Shoeshine Boys may be on the Yankees but the Joe Kennedys of the gambling world are on the other side, laying enough money down to force the books to drop the line.

A bettor who still likes New York is going to find himself in trouble. Do the Joe Kennedys win every single time? Of course not. Nevertheless, the numbers are certainly in their favor. Being on the same side as the sharps is a winning strategy over the long run.

# WHEN TO BET THE GAMES

There is often an internal battle over which way the line will move and if you should wait for a line to move in your favor. A bettor needs to use his own judgment and expertise to answer this. There are positives in getting your bet down early just as there are positives in waiting until game time before making your plays.

Each bet is an exercise in decision-making. With every decision, the longer you wait the more information you have. The main difficulty in decision-making is uncertainty. This uncertainty is reduced in baseball once you discover who the umpire will be, who is in the starting lineup, if any key players are banged up, what the bullpen situation may be, how the weather will be, and so on. The more you know about a game, the better you can measure the risk. Risk changes with each new development. It often is in the bettor's best interests to wait for as much information as he can get.

Betting early has its rewards, however. You may not know everything that you will know tomorrow, but an early bettor will get more of a virgin line. The value has not been bet out of it. You also complete your work. The knowledge that you are done handicapping has some great psychological benefits. Burnout when betting baseball can easily occur. Betting early will help avoid this potential. It will also avoid other possible problems. There is a tendency in baseball to get bogged down in minutiae, or in looking for that perfect betting opportunity. Just as it isn't too bright to spend 45 minutes in the mall parking lot waiting for the very best spot to open up, it isn't too bright waiting for more information if you don't need it. There is a fine line between too little and too much information. That final piece of the puzzle is rarely needed to discover the full picture. It can influence a bettor into ignoring older, more valuable news in favor of the new stuff.

There is no perfect time to place a bet on a game. Much depends on the process used to handicap, and your expectations regarding which way the line will move. If you notice the line always moving against you, it is probably in your best interests to wait. You will get a better price then. You can also use the time to check your work. Something isn't right with your handicapping if the line consistently moves away from your side.

If you are generally beating the line move, you will want to bet as quickly as possible. Over time, an alert bettor will choose correctly more often than not. Keeping detailed notes regarding line movement will help as well.

# HANDICAPPING THE MARKET

Some bettors handicap the teams while others handicap the market. Bettors who handicap the market pay little attention to who is playing who. They focus primarily on who is betting what. It is the Las Vegas version of "It's not what you know, it is who you know" These bettors spend all their effort studying line moves, trying to figure out what the sharp players are betting and tagging along.

There are some very vague assumptions that these "steam players" make:

- Professional bettors bet early
- The public bets late
- Early line moves tend to be sharp
- Late line moves tend to be from the public
- Extremely late line moves tend to come from sharps taking advantage of the late line moves from the public.

Sportsbooks will often over-react to steam, moving the line too far off the "right number". At this time, you may see these market handicappers jump in, buying the opposite side of the sharp money at a much better price. The assumption is that the initial lines makers know their stuff and the value has moved to the other side thanks to the steam.

One has to remember, however, that the people betting baseball are not the same crowd as the people betting football. For every five bettors playing the NFL, there may be one in baseball. And it isn't the sharper players who are sitting on the sidelines during the summer. The smart gamblers are still playing; the recreational bettor is finding something else to do with his time. Betting baseball on a daily basis is a lot more work than betting football on the weekends.

# LINES SERVICES

Vital to any steam chaser, lines services can save a bettor a great deal of hassle by keeping betting lines on one computer screen. Instead of logging in to all his different sportsbooks to get current odds, a bettor simply subscribes to a lines service. The first lines service was Don Best, formed in 1989 by Don Besssette before being sold to Al Corbo in 1992. Don Best initially featured lines from the Stardust, the Mirage, and the Riviera sportsbooks in Las Vegas. The company added the first offshore sportsbook in 1993. In 1997, the website was launched and Don Best immediately became a must have for sportsbooks and major bettors.

Don Best has been sold several times in recent years, most recently to Big Stick Media in 2008. While still thought by many to be the best service available, its high cost ($499 a month) and history of poor customer service has opened the door to other lines services.

Most notable of these services is SportsOptions.com. SportsOptions premium service costs $299 a month and offers real time odds for the majority of sportsbooks. The downside to SportsOptions is it doesn't offer real-time odds to all sportsbooks, in particular Bookmaker.com (where the line usually originates). However, Bookmaker is rarely worthwhile during baseball due to its 20-cent lines, wiping out this advantage for the baseball bettor.

What makes SportsOptions really stand out in the lines service market is the injury reports. SportsOptions has a team of employees on staff searching out game information and prides itself on being the first to announce injury news and lineup information. Information is money in sports betting, and being one of the first to know Mike Trout is sitting out a game more than makes up the cost of a lines service.

There are also several other free live lines services on the internet. To a smaller bettor who doesn't chase steam, these appear to work well enough. Baseball lines are relatively static, and the typical bettor will bet most of his action at the same handful of books.

It is the injury reports and lineup notices that set the premium lines services apart, however. If you plan to bet a lot of baseball, it is important to have one of the pay services. For my money, SportsOptions is the best. Both Don Best and SportsOptions offer a free trial period. If you wish to buy a service, make sure you test the two out first.

*Whether you think you can or you can't, you're right. – Henry Ford*

*Face reality as it is, not as it was or as you wish it to be. – Jack Welch*

# STATISTICS

The professor set some items down on his desk before philosophy class. When the bell rang, he wordlessly picked up a very large and very empty mayonnaise jar and proceeded to fill it with golf balls. He then asked the students if the jar was full. They agreed that it was.

The professor then picked up a box of marbles and poured them into the jar. He shook the jar lightly. The marbles rolled into the open areas between the golf balls. He again asked the students if the jar was full. They agreed it was.

Next came a bag of sand. The professor poured it into the jar. Of course, the sand filled up everything else. He asked once more if the jar was full. The students again answered, yes, the jar was full.

The professor then produced two beers from under the table and poured the entire contents into the jar effectively filling the empty space between the sand. The students laughed. The jar was definitely full now.

"This jar represents your life," said the professor as the laughter subsided. "The golf balls are the important things: Your family, your children, your health, and your friends. If everything else was lost and only they remained, your life would still be full. The marbles are the other things that matter: Your job, your hobbies, your house, and your car. The sand is everything else. The small stuff."

He went on. "If you put the sand into the jar first, there is no room for the marbles or the golf balls. The same goes for life. If you spend all your time and energy on the small stuff, you will never have room for the things that are important to you. Pay attention to the things that are critical to your happiness. Spend time with your children. Spend time with your parents. Visit with grandparents. Take your spouse out to dinner. Head to the lake. There will always be time to clean the house and mow the lawn. Take care of the golf balls first; the things that really matter. Set your priorities. The rest is just sand."

One of the students raised her hand and asked what the beer represented. The professor smiled and said, "I'm glad you asked." The beer shows you that no matter how full your life may seem, there's always room for a couple of drinks with a friend."

The sand that grinds us up in the real world will also grind up a bettor's gears if he fails to remember what the important stuff is when it comes to winning a game. We are bombarded with a wide range of statistics in today's baseball game. Obscure statistics like Relief Efficiency Rate and Ultimate Base Running provide some information to a bettor, but this statistic doesn't have much bearing on how a team will perform that day.

There are hundreds of these types of stats in the game today. The free access to data, and massive explosion in statistical interest since Michael Lewis's "Moneyball" was released, has resulted in a similarly explosion in new ways to measure players and teams. VORP (Value over Replacement Player) is now mainstream, at least to baseball fans. Win Shares is becoming an answer to the question of a player's worth. Win Probability Added uses play-by-play data to measure how much credit each player deserves for his team's victories. The list goes on and on. We can measure the spin of a pitch, the speed of a batted ball, and how quickly an outfielder reacts to a line drive. Do we want to know how well Detroit has hit against lefties in the last ten games? Or how the Tigers have hit on grass fields this year? Or at night? In a dome? Against a finesse pitcher? Against a fly-ball pitcher? It is all out there, and it is all free.

This wealth of information is certainly an improvement from years past for the average bettor. However, there is a great danger in getting bogged down in the minutia and forgetting the big picture. A statistic doesn't replace good judgment. It doesn't replace common sense. And it certainly doesn't replace sound money management.

There is a great desire among baseball bettors to find the one perfect statistic that will point the way to prosperity. It is time to give this dream up. There isn't one magic number out there. Some circumstances require a hammer. Some require a screwdriver. Betting at baseball (or any sport) requires flexibility and the understanding to know when the hammer is needed and when it isn't. Do we really care how bad a shortstop is defensively when a power pitcher like Max Scherzer is on the mound? Not really. Scherzer is a strikeout machine who might get a third of his outs via the strikeout. That isn't true when Rick Porcello was on the mound for Boston. A ground-ball pitcher without a strikeout pitch, Porcello needs a top defensive shortstop to be at his best.

To be of consequence to a handicapper, a statistic must primarily be useful in determining who wins or loses a baseball game. Nothing else. Stolen bases are one of those interesting historical statistics that fans, players, scouts, and announcers often use to judge the quality of a player, but it has little impact in predicting the outcome of a baseball game.

Only in hindsight is speed important to a gambler. If Juan Pierre bunts for a single, steals second base, then scores on two ground balls to break a 9th inning tie, speed will have made a difference. It is a waste of time, however, to handicap based on that possibility.

There are three conditions by which a statistic must be judged:

- It must be easy to understand. With fifteen games on the board every day, a statistic loses its purpose if it can't be used quickly and coherently.
- It must measure something important to winning a baseball game. Speed doesn't do this, so a team's stolen base information is irrelevant in most cases.
- It must accurately measure what it is trying to measure. A pitcher's record is one example. The pitcher's individual win-loss record is too heavily dependent on his team to have any basis in handicapping.

If a statistic doesn't meet these criteria, throw it out. You won't need it.

# MEASURING OFFENSE

"There is no clock in baseball". One often hears this particular argument in debates over the `quality' of a sport. This argument concerning baseball may be true in a technical sense. You obviously have seen the average time of a nine-inning game go up over the years. Nevertheless, it is false in an abstract sense of the word.

In baseball, the ticking clock doesn't measure time. It measures something far more scarce than minutes or seconds in a football game. The baseball clock measures outs. A team has three outs for an inning and 27 for a game. Its offensive abilities are measured against the backdrop of this ticking clock. If a batter gets on base, he succeeds. If he generates an out, he fails.

A team scores runs by putting batters on base and driving them in. The art needed in rating pitching is not required to judge offensive power: offense is for the most part simply math.

It is here we get into the nuts and bolts of measuring a team's offense. Getting on base is measured by on-base percentage. A bettor takes all the times a team gets on base, and divides that by how many times they are at bat. The linear equation is:

**OB%= (Hits plus Walks + Hit by Pitch) divided by (At bats plus Hit by Pitch + Sac Flies).**

The average on-base percentage for teams was .314 in 2014, with American League teams slightly higher due to the designated hitter rule. The extremes are sometimes severe: the Dodgers' on-base percentage was .333 while the Padres had an on-base percentage of just .292.

On base percentage tells us how often a team gets on base. However, an offense still must have the ability to drive that runner home. Slugging percentage is the best tool available to show us how well a team can do this. The equation for slugging percentage is:

**Slg% = (Hits plus Doubles + (Triples \*2) + (Homers \*3)) divided by ABs**

In 2014, the AL slugged .390 and the NL slugged .383.

To translate these two numbers into an understandable offensive power rating, I simply multiply a team's on-base percentage with its slugging percentage. This number is called OTS (on-base percentage TIMES slugging percentage) to differentiate it from OPS (on-base percentage PLUS slugging percentage that is now often used. OTS means nothing by itself. However, if I divide the team OTS by the league average OTS, I get something I can work with. The Orioles slugged .422 with a .311 on base percentage. Its raw OTS number, .131, divided by the league average OTS (.316\*.390=.123) equals 106%. Baltimore's offense is 6% above league average. The table below shows each American League team's OTS power number along with its runs scored power rating (runs scored per game divided by league average runs per game):

| Team | OBP | SLG | OTS | OTS/LG | RPG/LG |
|------|-----|-----|-----|--------|--------|
| Baltimore | .311 | .422 | .131 | 106% | 104% |
| Boston | .316 | .369 | .117 | 95% | 94% |
| Chicago White Sox | .310 | .398 | .123 | 100% | 97% |
| Cleveland | .317 | .389 | .123 | 100% | 99% |
| Detroit | .331 | .426 | .141 | 114% | 112% |
| Houston | .309 | .383 | .118 | 96% | 93% |
| Kansas City | .314 | .376 | .118 | 96% | 96% |
| LA Angels | .322 | .406 | .131 | 106% | 114% |
| Minnesota | .324 | .389 | .126 | 102% | 106% |
| NY Yankees | .307 | .380 | .117 | 95% | 94% |
| Oakland | .320 | .381 | .122 | 99% | 108% |
| Seattle | .300 | .376 | .113 | 92% | 94% |
| Tampa | .317 | .367 | .116 | 94% | 90% |
| Texas | .314 | .375 | .118 | 96% | 94% |
| Toronto | .323 | .414 | .134 | 109% | 107% |
| **League** | **.316** | **.390** | **.123** | **100%** | **100%** |

There are other offensive formulas developed in recent years that are slightly more accurate than the standard OTS formulas. Bill James, Clay Davenport, Keith Woolner, Phil Birnbaum, and Neil Bonner in particular deserve special mention for creating new statistics that measure a player's offensive contribution. Part of the problem with these formulas, however, is the degree of difficulty involved in the stat. The increased effort isn't worth the increase in accuracy.

The common availability of OTS also plays a large role in why I like the stat. Every website worth its salt has on base percentage and slugging percentage readily available. ESPN.com, Yahoo.com, MLB.com, and others also break these numbers down into different splits. When handicapping a team's offensive abilities, I look deeper than just raw OTS numbers. I want to know that team's OTS numbers on the road, at home, against righties, lefties, last twenty games, last fifty games, and so on.

By sticking with OTS, I am able to measure those factors. I can also determine if a team is getting "fluky" runs or not scoring at the rate its statistics would indicate. Oakland is one good example. Its OTS rating was 99%. Its actual run production was 108%, a significant difference.

A little investigation shows that the A's had a .400 slugging percentage with runners in scoring position compared to its overall slugging percentage of .354. That difference indicates Oakland had been very successful hitting in the clutch. Since clutch hitting, or lack of clutch hitting, is not a repeatable skill, Oakland's solid offensive performance in 2014 was more fluky than sustainable. Adjustments are made during the season to account for this.

# FACTORING FOR PLATOON SPLITS

The theory of platooning has gone through various stages over the years. In 1914, the Red Sox won a World Series thanks to its platoon system. Many major league baseball teams saw the effect and followed suit. Platooning gradually began to fade out around the peak of the Babe Ruth years for a variety of reasons, chief among them resistance from players. Not until Casey Stengel was hired in New York did the platoon system come back in vogue. Earl Weaver began keeping detailed records of pitcher/hitter matchups and made journeymen like John Lowenstein and Elrod Hendricks into productive major league hitters. Tony LaRussa took it even further, keeping numerous left-handed pitchers in the bullpen solely to take advantage of the lefty-lefty matchups that favor pitchers.

Winning bettors consider this when making plays. However, just as there is a risk in ignoring platoon splits, there is also a big risk in over-adjusting for it as well. The platoon factor is real; almost all right-handed hitters hit better against lefties than they do against right-handed pitchers. The same holds true on the other side of the plate as well. Lefties hit better against their opposite number compared to how well they do against fellow left-handers.

These differences can be measured relatively accurately. RH batters historically hit 9% better against lefties than versus righties. This number has been constant for 50 plus years. Hitters who may have pounded lefties for one season will likely revert to this 9% spread the next season. A right-handed hitter's platoon splits has no predictive value for the next season. If you want to find out how well a RH batter will hit lefties, the best way is to determine how he hits righties.

LH batters are a bit different. Whereas right-handed hitters who can't hit RH pitchers are weeded out of baseball in the minor leagues, many left-handed hitters are able to advance through the system without facing high quality left-handed pitchers. Some learn how to hit them, and others don't. Unlike RH batters, there are very large, persistent platoon splits among some lefties. Still, you can't just look at how a lefty has hit against LH pitchers to forecast how he will hit lefties in the future. You have to look at how well he hits against right-handers as well.

It is important to note which team is loaded with left-handed batters and check their platoon splits. These teams are more vulnerable to a platoon effect than teams more righty centric.

There were a handful of teams that had exploitable splits in 2014. The Braves hit much better against lefties. Texas likewise was much better against lefties compared to righties. The Pirates had the opposite split, pounding right-handed pitching while having big problems versus lefties. There is no guarantee that these trends will continue in 2015. Teams know when they are unbalanced on offense and have an entire off-season to fix the problem. However, balancing your roster is harder to do during the season, and handicappers will find it profitable to keep an eye out for teams with heavy splits.

Like hitters, pitchers can have huge platoon splits. Right-handed pitchers Roberto Hernandez, Ubaldo Jimenez, Tim Lincecum, and Zack Wheeler all dominated right-handed hitters but struggled against lefties. Alex Wood, Wei Yin Chen, Zach McAllister, and Henderson Alvarez did better against lefties compared to right-handers.

*In the realm of ideas, everything depends on enthusiasm. In the real world, all rests on perseverance. – Johann Wolfgang von Goethe*


*A man must be big enough to admit his mistakes, smart enough to profit from them, and strong enough to correct them. – John C. Maxwell*

# 2014 MLB TEAM SPLITS

| TEAM | vs LH | OBP | SLG | OTS/Lg | vs RH | SLG | OPS | OTS/Lg |
|---|---|---|---|---|---|---|---|---|
| Arizona | | .307 | .364 | 90% | | .379 | .679 | 96% |
| Atlanta | | .330 | .382 | 102% | | .354 | .651 | 86% |
| Baltimore | | .310 | .428 | 107% | | .420 | .732 | 114% |
| Boston | | .314 | .375 | 95% | | .366 | .682 | 93% |
| Cubs | | .324 | .401 | 105% | | .379 | .671 | 94% |
| White Sox | | .308 | .409 | 102% | | .394 | .705 | 103% |
| Cincinnati | | .297 | .378 | 91% | | .361 | .657 | 88% |
| Cleveland | | .312 | .360 | 91% | | .402 | .722 | 108% |
| Colorado | | .334 | .462 | 125% | | .439 | .763 | 124% |
| Detroit | | .339 | .451 | 124% | | .417 | .745 | 115% |
| Houston | | .334 | .413 | 112% | | .372 | .673 | 93% |
| Kansas City | | .322 | .387 | 101% | | .372 | .682 | 94% |
| LA Angels | | .336 | .427 | 116% | | .399 | .716 | 106% |
| LA Dodgers | | .329 | .387 | 103% | | .412 | .746 | 114% |
| Miami | | .320 | .389 | 101% | | .374 | .690 | 96% |
| Milwaukee | | .304 | .401 | 99% | | .396 | .708 | 104% |
| Minnesota | | .323 | .385 | 101% | | .391 | .715 | 104% |
| NY Mets | | .305 | .328 | 81% | | .376 | .685 | 96% |
| NY Yankees | | .320 | .393 | 102% | | .375 | .677 | 94% |
| Oakland | | .313 | .368 | 93% | | .386 | .708 | 101% |
| Philadelphia | | .301 | .373 | 91% | | .359 | .662 | 88% |
| Pittsburgh | | .322 | .370 | 96% | | .414 | .746 | 115% |
| San Diego | | .289 | .326 | 76% | | .347 | .640 | 82% |
| San Fran | | .318 | .390 | 100% | | .387 | .695 | 100% |
| Seattle | | .294 | .342 | 81% | | .394 | .697 | 102% |
| St. Louis | | .330 | .388 | 104% | | .363 | .679 | 91% |
| Tampa Bay | | .316 | .377 | 96% | | .363 | .681 | 92% |
| Texas | | .339 | .416 | 114% | | .360 | .664 | 89% |
| Toronto | | .311 | .389 | 98% | | .423 | .750 | 118% |
| Washington | | .329 | .399 | 106% | | .391 | .709 | 103% |
| **Average** | | **.318** | **.389** | **100%** | | **.386** | **.698** | **100%** |

# EXPLOITING DEFENSE

When a surprise team busts out of the gates early in the season, one key factor could be the team's defense. Offense is usually predictable and easy to forecast. A team averaging six runs a game is going to do pretty well. Not so with pitching. A pitcher with a 3.70 ERA may be good, lucky, or have a great defense behind him. In baseball, what we often think is good pitching may simply be good defense.

An elite pitcher like Clayton Kershaw can create his own outs by striking out batters. Lower class pitchers like Scott Feldman or Jeremy Guthrie are forced to use their defense to get outs, leaving these types of pitchers vulnerable to poor defense.

The quickest way to measure the quality of a team's defense is the Defensive Efficiency Ratio developed by Bill James. DER is a formula that calculates how often a ball hit into the field of play is turned into an out:

**1 - ((Hits Allowed - Homers Allowed) / (ABs - Strikeouts - Homers))**

The average rate for a team is usually around 69%. In other words, a ball hit into the field of play will be turned into an out 69% of the time. Teams with a higher number typically help its pitching staff; a rate under 69% means a pitcher is getting hurt by his defense.

The best defense in the major leagues last year was the Oakland A's. The A's defense turned 72.8% of its opportunities into outs. Less base runners, less runs scored. The Giants were the one of the best defensive team in the National League, a large reason why this under the radar team won the World Series last season.

Some teams don't care much about DER and other defensive rating systems. Or at least they don't trust them. The Twins GM signed poor fielding right fielder Torii Hunter and said, "When you look at the rankings of the defensive side of the game, you shake your head many times. I'm not saying a lot of them aren't accurate, because some of them are, but a lot of them aren't accurate either."

Minnesota had the lowest DER rating in the AL, and had the worst ERA in the league as well. The same hold true for the Diamondbacks as well. Arizona's 68.8% DER was the worst in the National League; only the Rockies and Coors Field kept Arizona and its 4.58 ERA from the bottom of the barrel in the NL.

| TEAM | DER | Rank | Runs/Game | Rank |
|------|-----|------|-----------|------|
| OAK | .728 | 1 | 3.22 | 3 |
| SEA | .725 | 2 | 3.17 | 2 |
| CIN | .723 | 3 | 3.59 | 16 |
| BAL | .720 | 4 | 3.44 | 7 |
| SFN | .718 | 5 | 3.50 | 10 |
| ANA | .715 | 6 | 3.58 | 15 |
| SLN | .714 | 7 | 3.50 | 10 |
| TBA | .714 | 7 | 3.56 | 13 |
| MIL | .711 | 9 | 3.67 | 17 |
| SDN | .711 | 9 | 3.27 | 4 |
| PIT | .710 | 11 | 3.49 | 8 |
| KCA | .708 | 12 | 3.51 | 12 |
| LAN | .707 | 13 | 3.40 | 6 |
| TOR | .706 | 14 | 4.00 | 22 |
| WAS | .706 | 14 | 3.03 | 1 |
| NYN | .705 | 16 | 3.49 | 8 |
| PHI | .705 | 16 | 3.81 | 20 |
| NYA | .702 | 18 | 3.75 | 18 |
| HOU | .701 | 19 | 4.14 | 25 |
| ATL | .700 | 20 | 3.38 | 5 |
| BOS | .699 | 21 | 4.01 | 23 |
| CHN | .696 | 22 | 3.92 | 21 |
| CHA | .694 | 23 | 4.27 | 27 |
| COL | .693 | 24 | 4.86 | 30 |
| CLE | .691 | 25 | 3.57 | 14 |
| MIA | .690 | 26 | 3.79 | 19 |

| TEAM | DER | Rank | Runs/Game | Rank |
|------|------|------|-----------|------|
| TEX | .690 | 26 | 4.49 | 28 |
| ARI | .688 | 28 | 4.26 | 26 |
| DET | .688 | 28 | 4.01 | 23 |
| MIN | .685 | 30 | 4.58 | 29 |

As a crude but passable rule of thumb, each 1% difference in team DER is worth five cents to a bettor. It is just a rule of thumb. Park factors matter. Colorado's large field of play makes it is more difficult to turn a batted ball into an out. Baseball Prospectus has a tool called "PADE" that makes adjustments due to park factors. The defensive ability of a team can also change drastically from season to season, week to week, and game to game. As injuries take their toll, and players get days off or shipped out, the defense quality of a team can fluctuate greatly.

# MELTDOWNS

In most cases, it is silly to change power ratings of teams that hit a little slump or get on a hot streak. Streaks happen and over-reacting means a bettor will sell low and buy high. Nevertheless, some instances demand a change in perspective:

- A team is losing consistently as a favorite.
- A team's manager is under fire
- A team is having problems with its fans and media
- A team expected to contend for the division title is mired in a slump behind the leaders.

When teams are having these problems, wait it out before betting on them. The team should rebound if they are playing beneath their level of talent. However, dumping good money after bad doesn't make sense during a meltdown. There is no reason to ride them until they start showing a little life.

# THE PITCHER'S TOOLBOX

A handicapper can use a wide range of tools to determine the expected performance level of a starting pitcher. None tells the whole story but each adds a piece to the puzzle we are constantly trying to solve. Some of these include:

## EARNED RUN AVERAGE

The most common statistic is the Earned Run Average (ERA). The ERA is the number of earned runs a pitcher allows per nine innings on the mound. To determine a pitcher's ERA, you multiply the total earned runs by nine then divides that total by the number of innings pitched. The American League ERA in 2014 was 3.81; in the National League, it was 3.66. Scoring in both leagues decreased sharply from the 2009 season. In 2013, the NL ERA was 3.73 ERA and the AL's ERA was 3.99.

The ERA has too many flaws to be much use as a handicapping tool. The most obvious one is its failure to account for a starter's relief pitching. If a pitcher is pulled from the game with the bases loaded and one out, that pitcher may not get charged with an earned run if the relief pitcher does his job. If the reliever melts down, the starter gets charged with all three runs. Both circumstances were out of the starter's control, but its impact on his ERA is heavy.

It isn't worthless, however. The ERA is used by everyone as a quick reference to a pitcher's quality. If someone says a pitcher's ERA is 3.00, I know immediately that the pitcher is probably pretty good. You can't say that about WHIP or the various other new statistics. ERA, even with its flaws, serves a good purpose. I often use a pitcher's ERA to illustrate a point, but many more other tools are available to show a pitcher's skill.

# EXPECTED ERA (xERA)

xERA is a tool used to take some of the "noise" away from a pitcher's earned run average. A pitcher's xERA isn't affected by his bullpen support or defense. The formula for xERA is:

| Step 1 | | .575 * Hits Allowed Per Nine Innings |
|--------|-------|------------------------------------------|
| Step 2 | Plus  | .94 * Home Runs Allowed Per Nine |
| Step 3 | Plus  | .28 * Walks Allowed Per Nine |
| Step 4 | Minus | .01 * Strikeouts Per Nine |
| Step 5 | Minus | 2.68 |

xERA is usually in the same neighborhood as a pitcher's true ERA. When there is a difference in the two numbers, however, a bettor should be prepared to dig deeper into the pitcher's performance. Differences less than half a run are discounted; differences greater than .50 indicates a possibility of betting on or against the pitcher. When given a choice between ERA and xERA, choose xERA. This number is more accurate regarding future performance than a pitcher's true ERA.

If a pitcher's xERA is higher than his actual ERA, then he got a bit lucky. His ERA will likely rise. If his xERA is lower than his ERA, then the pitcher threw better than the numbers indicate. He may be undervalued when the line is made.

## FIELDING INDEPENDENT PITCHING (FIP) ERA

Similar to the above formula, FIP ERA was designed to measure only the variables that the pitcher completely controls. Tom Tango, co-author of The Book, developed this formula. It assumes pitchers have control over only home runs, strikeouts, and walks. Everything else...base hits, errors, runs, can be chalked up to random chance. FIP ERA tells you how well the pitcher pitched, regardless of how well his fielders fielded.

FIP ERA= ((HR*13) + ((BB+HBP)*3) − (K's *2) / Innings pitched) +3.20

| Step 1 | | Home Runs *13 |
|--------|-----------|----------------------------|
| Step 2 | Plus | (Walks Plus Hit Batters) *3 |
| Step 3 | Minus | Strikeouts * 2 |
| Step 4 | Divided by | Innings Pitched |
| Step 5 | Plus | 3.2 |

The 3.2 number in step 5 is a constant designed to make the FIP number similar to an ERA. It will vary slightly from year to year.

The FIP and ERA will rarely match up perfectly with each other. Small differences are ignored; what you are looking for is larger differences over .35. A 3.70 ERA and 3.80 FIP are essentially the same. A 3.70 ERA and 4.20 FIP means something isn't matching up and needs to be investigated.

One negative to FIP ERA is the heavy influence home runs have on the number. A pitcher's home run rate varies from year to year so one must be careful when to apply this. FIP can also be tweaked by replacing the pitcher's home run rate to the league average home run per fly ball rate. This adjustment, called xFIP, tends to be a better predictor of a pitcher's future performance. If you have to choose one and only one statistic to forecast a pitcher's future, xFIP is it.


### DEFENSE INDEPENDENT PITCHING STATS (DIPS) ERA

The father to FIP ERA, DIPS ERA was created by Voros McCracken. It is a complicated formula, designed by McCracken to show that pitchers have far less impact on turning batted balls into outs than previously thought. McCracken's work was the jumping off point to many great pitching tool, but DIPS ERA is too complicated to be of much direct use in handicapping.

# POWER/FINESSE RATING

This formula determines how reliant a pitcher is on his defense. It measures how often a pitcher allows balls to be hit into the field of play. Finesse pitchers need a good defense behind them to succeed. Power pitchers can get away with having a bad defense. The formula:

(WALKS PLUS STRIKEOUTS) DIVIDED BY INNINGS PITCHED

A rating above 1.10 denotes a power pitcher. The fourteen starting pitchers with the highest Power/Finesse rating are listed below:

| Name | P/F Rate | Name | P/F Rate |
|---|---|---|---|
| Francisco Liriano | 1.58 | Clayton Kershaw | 1.36 |
| Zack Wheeler | 1.44 | Corey Kluber | 1.36 |
| Max Scherzer | 1.43 | C.J. Wilson | 1.35 |
| Chris Sale | 1.42 | A.J. Burnett | 1.34 |
| Jake Odorizzi | 1.39 | Stephen Strasburg | 1.33 |
| Ian Kennedy | 1.38 | Drew Hutchison | 1.32 |
| Tyson Ross | 1.37 | Wade Miley | 1.28 |

The fourteen starting pitchers with the lowest Power/Finesse rating in 2014 are listed below. These pitchers are vulnerable to poor defense:

| Name | P/F Rate | Name | P/F Rate |
|---|---|---|---|
| Doug Fister | .74 | Scott Feldman | .87 |
| Henderson Alvarez | .77 | Eric Stults | .89 |
| Tim Hudson | .81 | Tanner Roark | .89 |
| Mark Buehrle | .82 | Kyle Kendrick | .89 |
| Rick Porcello | .83 | Bartolo Colon | .90 |
| Jeremy Guthrie | .86 | Jason Vargas | .90 |
| Josh Collmenter | .86 | Hiroki Kuroda | .91 |

Other pitching tools that help a bettor determine the talent level of a pitcher:

## WALKS/HITS RATIO (WHIP)

The formula is simple: add the walks and hits together, and divide by innings pitched. Look on WHIP as a form of a pitcher's On Base Percentage. A 1.20 WHIP is very good; a 1.50 WHIP means the pitcher is walking a thin line.

## GROUND BALL PITCHERS

Taken as a group, ground ball pitchers give up more hits and strike out fewer batters than fly ball pitchers. That doesn't mean they are less effective, however. While ground ball pitchers allow more base runners than the typical fly-ball pitcher, they also give up fewer home runs. The best way to determine a pitcher's ground ball tendencies is obviously his ground ball rate. 42% is league average. Anything above 50% is good, while anything below 35% means the pitcher is prone to giving up an ill-time home run. The chart below lists the most extreme ground ball pitchers in 2014 and their home run rates per nine innings:

| Name | GB Rate | Name | GB Rate |
|---|---|---|---|
| Dallas Keuchel | 63.5% | Jarred Cosart | 54.2% |
| Tyson Ross | 57.0% | Zack Wheeler | 54.0% |
| Felix Hernandez | 56.2% | Henderson Alvarez | 53.8% |
| Alex Cobb | 56.2% | Wily Peralta | 53.6% |
| Sonny Gray | 55.9% | Mike Leake | 53.4% |
| Francisco Liriano | 54.4% | Tim Hudson | 53.1% |
| Kyle Gibson | 54.4% | Jarred Cosart | 54.2% |

## FLYBALL PITCHERS

Fly ball pitchers are far more affected by weather and ballpark than ground ball pitchers: you certainly don't want to bet on Chris Young when the wind is blowing out to center field in Wrigley Park.

Nevertheless, at home in San Diego, Chris Young is a very effective pitcher. Those fly balls that might land in the seats at Wrigley instead are caught on the warning track at Petco Field. In general, fly ball pitchers are more prone to struggle unless the pitcher has the ability to get strikeouts or a ballpark to cover up his mistakes in the strike zone. Keep an eye out for pitchers with a fly ball rate over 40% if they can't get strikeouts. The chart below lists the most extreme fly-ball pitchers and their home run rates.

| Name | FB% | Name | Fly Rate |
|---|---|---|---|
| Chris Young | 59% | Jake Peavy | 42% |
| Jake Odorizzi | 49% | Max Scherzer | 42% |
| Jered Weaver | 48% | Shelby Miller | 41% |
| Drew Hutchison | 45% | Chris Sale | 41% |
| Colby Lewis | 44% | Kyle Lohse | 41% |
| Julio Teheran | 44% | Justin Verlander | 41% |
| Travis Wood | 42% | Hector Noesi | 41% |

## COMMAND RATE

The command rate is calculated by dividing strikeouts by walks. A few years back, a 2.0 ratio meant the pitcher was decent. That's not the case in today's game, however. The best pitchers will have a 3.0 ratio at a minimum. These pitchers, even when struggling, will likely show a sharp rate of improvement over the short and long term. A starting pitcher with a 2.0 ratio is now in the bottom 20% of the pitching pool and treading dangerous waters.

The command rate is not perfect; it weighs strikeouts and walks equally, and tends to overvalue junk ballers who give up a ton of hits but walk few batters. A pitcher that walks two and strikes out seven is more impressive than a pitcher that walks only one and strikes out four. The command rate says differently, but this is a case where common sense should overrule an otherwise solid statistic. Once a bettor accounts for these exceptions, the command rate is an extremely effective tool.

| Name | Command | Name | Command |
|---|---|---|---|
| Phil Hughes | 11.6 | Chris Sale | 5.3 |
| Clayton Kershaw | 7.7 | Brandon McCarthy | 5.3 |
| Hisashi Iwakuma | 7.3 | Corey Kluber | 5.3 |
| David Price | 7.1 | Madison Bumgarner | 5.1 |
| Jordan Zimmermann | 6.3 | Bartolo Colon | 5.0 |
| Stephen Strasburg | 5.6 | Zack Greinke | 4.8 |
| Felix Hernandez | 5.4 | Jeff Samardzija | 4.7 |

## DOMINANCE (K/9)

A pitcher's ability to create outs on his own is called Dominance. The formula for Dominance is strikeouts divided by innings pitched multiplied by nine.

There is a school of thought in baseball that a strikeout is just another out. A batter whose 300 outs in a season include 180 strikeouts does not hurt his team any more than a batter who strikes out 40 times while making the same 300 outs. That is not the case. When a batter makes contact with a pitch, anything can happen. When a batter strikes out, nothing happens but a slow trip back to the dugout.

Strikeouts show how well a pitcher can dominate a game. About 70% of all batted balls fall in for base hits. Strikeouts eliminate this possibility, and allow a pitcher to escape the errors, bloopers, and broken bat singles that typically plague pitchers.

Chris Sale had 208 strikeouts in 174 regular season innings in 2014. His Dominance rate works out to be 208 / 174 * 9 = 10.8. The most dominant pitchers will have Dominance rates over nine while the least dominant will have a rate under five. The typical starter will have a Dominance rate around 7.

| Pitcher | K/9 | Pitcher | K/9 |
|---|---|---|---|
| Clayton Kershaw | 10.9 | Francisco Liriano | 9.7 |
| Chris Sale | 10.8 | Felix Hernandez | 9.5 |
| Max Scherzer | 10.3 | Jake Odorizzi | 9.3 |
| Corey Kluber | 10.3 | Ian Kennedy | 9.3 |
| Stephen Strasburg | 10.1 | Zack Greinke | 9.2 |
| David Price | 9.8 | Zack Wheeler | 9.1 |
| Francisco Liriano | 9.7 | Madison Bumgarner | 9.1 |

## STRIKEOUT PERCENTAGE

The strikeout percentage statistic doesn't get the attention given to a pitcher's K/9 rate, but it is a more reliable gage of a pitcher's ability to strike out batters. The formula is simple: number of strikeouts divided by the number of batters faced. In most cases, the K/9 and K% will be similar. Clayton Kershaw and Chris Sale were the top two pitchers in 2014 in both categories. However, there are some exceptions. Pitchers who walk a lot of batters or give up a lot of hits over the course of the year had more chances to strike out batters. K% accounts for that.

| Pitcher | K% | Pitcher | K% |
|---|---|---|---|
| Clayton Kershaw | 31.9% | David Price | 26.9% |
| Chris Sale | 30.4% | Francisco Liriano | 25.3% |
| Corey Kluber | 28.3% | Johnny Cueto | 25.2% |
| Stephen Strasburg | 27.9% | Zack Greinke | 25.2% |
| Max Scherzer | 27.9% | Madison Bumgarner | 25.1% |
| Felix Hernandez | 27.2% | Jon Lester | 24.9% |

| Pitcher | K% | Pitcher | K% |
|---|---|---|---|
| Mark Buehrle | 13.9% | Roberto Hernandez | 14.5% |
| Scott Feldman | 14.0% | Eric Stults | 14.6% |
| Kyle Kendrick | 14.0% | Doug Fister | 14.8% |
| Kyle Gibson | 14.1% | Jarred Cosart | 15.0% |
| Henderson Alvarez | 14.4% | John Danks | 15.1% |
| Jeremy Guthrie | 14.4% | Tim Hudson | 15.2% |

# CONTROL RATE

The control rate is walks divided by innings pitched multiplied by nine. This number will show you the pitcher's ability to throw the ball over the plate. You are looking for pitchers that have a control rate less than 2.7. A starter with the ability to strikeout batters will often be able to overcome a bad control rate, but it is a thin line to walk.

## Worst control rate 2014:

| Pitcher | BB/9 | Pitcher | BB/9 |
|---|---|---|---|
| Francisco Liriano | 4.49 | Jarred Cosart | 3.64 |
| C.J. Wilson | 4.35 | Shelby Miller | 3.59 |
| A.J. Burnett | 4.04 | Roenis Elias | 3.52 |
| Roberto Hernandez | 3.99 | John Danks | 3.44 |
| Travis Wood | 3.94 | Yordano Ventura | 3.39 |
| Zack Wheeler | 3.84 | Wade Miley | 3.35 |

## Best control rate in 2014:

| Pitcher | BB/9 | Pitcher | BB/9 |
|---|---|---|---|
| Phil Hughes | 0.69 | Clayton Kershaw | 1.41 |
| Hisashi Iwakuma | 1.06 | Brandon McCarthy | 1.49 |
| Jordan Zimmermann | 1.31 | Hiroki Kuroda | 1.58 |
| Doug Fister | 1.32 | Henderson Alvarez | 1.59 |
| Bartolo Colon | 1.33 | Tim Hudson | 1.62 |
| David Price | 1.38 | Wei-Yin Chen | 1.70 |

# WALK PERCENTAGE

The Walk Percentage formula is walks allowed divided by batters faced. It is similar to the Control Rate stat and should line up closely with it.

| Pitcher | BB% | Pitcher | BB% |
|---|---|---|---|
| Francisco Liriano | 11.7% | Shelby Miller | 9.6% |
| C.J. Wilson | 11.2% | Jarred Cosart | 9.5% |

| A.J. Burnett | 10.3% | Roenis Elias | 9.2% |
|---|---|---|---|
| Roberto Hernandez | 10.1% | Tyson Ross | 8.9% |
| Zack Wheeler | 10.0% | Edinson Volquez | 8.8% |
| Travis Wood | 9.7% | Chris Archer | 8.8% |

## Lowest Walk%

| Pitcher | BB% | Pitcher | BB% |
|---|---|---|---|
| Phil Hughes | 1.9% | Brandon McCarthy | 4.0% |
| Hisashi Iwakuma | 3.0% | Clayton Kershaw | 4.1% |
| Jordan Zimmermann | 3.6% | Hiroki Kuroda | 4.3% |
| Doug Fister | 3.6% | Henderson Alvarez | 4.3% |
| Bartolo Colon | 3.6% | Tim Hudson | 4.3% |
| David Price | 3.8% | Wei-Yin Chen | 4.5% |

## BATTING AVERAGE ON BALLS IN PLAY (BABIP)
(Hits – Home runs)
Divided by
(At bats – strikeouts – home runs + sacrifice flies)

This statistic, also known as Hit Rate, measures how many balls in play against a pitcher fall in for hits. BABIP is used as a red flag in sabermetric analysis; a consistently high or low BABIP is hard for pitchers to maintain. A high BABIP means the pitcher was unlucky and should improve. A low BABIP means the pitcher can be expected to decline. Knuckleballers like RA Dickey are an exception to this rule. The league average is around .300.

### Lowest BABIP

| Pitcher | BABIP | Pitcher | BABIP |
|---|---|---|---|
| Chris Young | .238 | R.A. Dickey | .263 |
| Johnny Cueto | .238 | Jorge de la Rosa | .263 |
| Shelby Miller | .256 | Garrett Richards | .264 |
| Felix Hernandez | .258 | Alfredo Simon | .265 |
| Doug Fister | .262 | Roberto Hernandez | .266 |
| Edinson Volquez | .263 | Adam Wainwright | .267 |

## Highest BABIP

| Pitcher | BABIP | Pitcher | BABIP |
|---|---|---|---|
| Colby Lewis | .339 | Jose Quintana | .318 |
| Brandon McCarthy | .328 | Aaron Harang | .318 |
| Phil Hughes | .324 | Justin Verlander | .317 |
| Nathan Eovaldi | .323 | Wade Miley | .317 |
| Travis Wood | .320 | Mark Buehrle | .316 |
| Ervin Santana | .319 | Corey Kluber | .316 |

## STRAND RATE

(Hits + walks –earned runs)  Divided by
(Hits + walks – home runs)

Created by Ron Shandler, the strand rate measures the percentage of allowed runners a pitcher strands. The higher it is, the more fortunate the pitcher was over the course of the season.

### Highest Strand Rate

| Gonzalez, Miguel | 82% | Hernandez, Felix | 80% |
|---|---|---|---|
| Lester, Jon | 81% | Darvish, Yu | 79% |
| Sale, Chris | 81% | Tanaka, Masahiro | 79% |
| Duffy, Danny | 81% | House, T.J. | 78% |
| Pineda, Michael | 81% | Chavez, Jesse | 78% |
| Kluber, Corey | 80% | Ventura, Yordano | 77% |

### Lowest strand rate

| Buchholz, Clay | 62% | Hutchison, Drew | 67% |
|---|---|---|---|
| McAllister, Zach | 63% | Sanchez, Anibal | 67% |
| Workman, Brandon | 65% | Tomlin, Josh | 68% |
| Skaggs, Tyler | 65% | Verlander, Justin | 68% |
| Gibson, Kyle | 65% | Stroman, Marcus | 68% |
| Nolasco, Ricky | 67% | Lewis, Colby | 69% |

# HOME RUNS PER FLY BALL

On average, 10% of all fly balls are home runs. A pitcher like Garrett Richards gave up a home run on only 3.9% of his fly balls, indicating he was fortunate in 2014. Brandon McCarthy was on the other end of the scale. Pitchers don't have much control over the number of fly balls that turn into home runs; it will typically trend back to the 10% number.

### Best Home Run Rate

| Pitcher | HR/FB | | Pitcher | HR/FB |
|---------|-------|---|---------|-------|
| Garrett Richards | 3.9% | | Aaron Harang | 6.4% |
| Jose Quintana | 5.1% | | Jordan Zimmermann | 6.4% |
| Adam Wainwright | 5.3% | | Nathan Eovaldi | 6.6% |
| Jarred Cosart | 6.0% | | Mark Buehrle | 6.6% |
| Lance Lynn | 6.1% | | Clayton Kershaw | 6.6% |
| Phil Hughes | 6.2% | | Justin Verlander | 6.8% |

### Worst Home Run Rate

| Pitcher | HR/FB | | Pitcher | HR/FB |
|---------|-------|---|---------|-------|
| Brandon McCarthy | 16.3% | | Jorge de la Rosa | 12.9% |
| Wade Miley | 13.9% | | Hector Noesi | 12.7% |
| Wily Peralta | 13.9% | | Eric Stults | 12.5% |
| Hisashi Iwakuma | 13.2% | | Roberto Hernandez | 12.2% |
| Stephen Strasburg | 13.1% | | Yovani Gallardo | 12.1% |
| Mike Leake | 13.1% | | Jason Hammel | 12.0% |

# Outside the Zone Swing Rate

Plate discipline is vital for a hitter, and a pitcher who gets a batter to swing at a pitch outside the strike zone is ahead of the game when it comes to the pitcher/hitter battle. The MLB average is 30%. The leaderboard for this category is littered with elite pitchers.

## Best Rate

| Pitcher | O-Swg% | | | Pitcher | O-Swg% |
|---|---|---|---|---|---|
| Phil Hughes | .380 | | | Stephen Strasburg | .363 |
| Brandon McCarthy | .374 | | | Madison Bumgarner | .362 |
| Clayton Kershaw | .370 | | | Corey Kluber | .356 |
| Jordan Zimmermann | .369 | | | Johnny Cueto | .356 |
| Alex Cobb | .368 | | | Hisashi Iwakuma | .355 |
| Zack Greinke | .367 | | | John Lackey | .354 |

## Worst Rate

| Pitcher | O-Swg% | | | Pitcher | O-Swg% |
|---|---|---|---|---|---|
| C.J. Wilson | .234 | | | Yovani Gallardo | .274 |
| A.J. Burnett | .255 | | | Edinson Volquez | .277 |
| Shelby Miller | .259 | | | Jarred Cosart | .277 |
| Chris Tillman | .267 | | | Jon Niese | .279 |
| Jered Weaver | .268 | | | Zack Wheeler | .280 |
| Tom Koehler | .273 | | | Travis Wood | .282 |

# Contact Percentage

The overall percentage of a batter makes contact with when swinging the bat. MLB average is 81%. The lower the contact rate, the better.

## Lowest Contact Rate

| Pitcher | Contact% | | | Pitcher | Contact% |
|---|---|---|---|---|---|
| Francisco Liriano | 68% | | | Ervin Santana | 75% |
| Tyson Ross | 71% | | | Max Scherzer | 75% |
| Clayton Kershaw | 73% | | | Zack Greinke | 76% |
| Chris Sale | 73% | | | Garrett Richards | 76% |
| Felix Hernandez | 74% | | | Cole Hamels | 76% |
| Corey Kluber | 74% | | | Stephen Strasburg | 76% |

## Highest Contact Rate

| Pitcher | Contact% | | Pitcher | Contact% |
|---|---|---|---|---|
| Bartolo Colon | 88% | | Chris Tillman | 85% |
| Doug Fister | 87% | | Colby Lewis | 85% |
| Mark Buehrle | 86% | | Phil Hughes | 84% |
| Scott Feldman | 86% | | Jeremy Guthrie | 84% |
| Travis Wood | 86% | | Jarred Cosart | 84% |
| Henderson Alvarez | 85% | | Chris Young | 84% |

# Swinging Strike Percentage

The percentage of total pitches a batter swings and misses on. This statistic is a clear indication about a pitcher's stuff and ability to dominate games. A pitcher with a low swinging strike percentage is reliant on his defense and prone to big innings.

## Best Swinging Strike Rate

| Pitcher | SwStr% | | Pitcher | SwStr% |
|---|---|---|---|---|
| Clayton Kershaw | 14.1% | | Felix Hernandez | 11.8% |
| Francisco Liriano | 13.6% | | Ervin Santana | 11.7% |
| Chris Sale | 12.9% | | Zack Greinke | 11.6% |
| Tyson Ross | 12.5% | | Max Scherzer | 11.5% |
| Corey Kluber | 11.9% | | Stephen Strasburg | 11.2% |
| Cole Hamels | 11.9% | | Madison Bumgarner | 11.1% |

## Worst Swinging Strike Rate

| Pitcher | SwStr% | | Pitcher | SwStr% |
|---|---|---|---|---|
| Bartolo Colon | 5.6% | | Colby Lewis | 6.9% |
| Doug Fister | 6.1% | | Mike Leake | 6.9% |
| Scott Feldman | 6.1% | | Chris Tillman | 6.9% |
| Mark Buehrle | 6.3% | | Yovani Gallardo | 6.9% |
| Travis Wood | 6.5% | | Dan Haren | 7.0% |
| Jarred Cosart | 6.6% | | Shelby Miller | 7.0% |

# Pace

How long between pitches a pitcher typically takes. This stat doesn't have an impact on handicapping, but games with Price or Buchholz on the mound usually are as interesting as watching paint dry. Buehrle always works fast.

## Slowest Pace (in seconds)

| Name | Pace | | Pitcher | Pace |
|---|---|---|---|---|
| David Price | 26.6 | | Zack Greinke | 24.8 |
| Jorge de la Rosa | 26.0 | | Hisashi Iwakuma | 24.7 |
| Clay Buchholz | 25.6 | | Matt Garza | 24.7 |
| Edinson Volquez | 25.3 | | Ryan Vogelsong | 24.7 |
| Hiroki Kuroda | 25.2 | | Alex Cobb | 24.5 |
| Chris Archer | 25.2 | | Corey Kluber | 24.4 |

## Fastest Pace

| Name | Pace | | Pitcher | Pace |
|---|---|---|---|---|
| Mark Buehrle | 17.3 | | Chris Young | 19.8 |
| R.A. Dickey | 18.3 | | Eric Stults | 19.9 |
| Doug Fister | 18.5 | | John Danks | 19.9 |
| Wade Miley | 19.0 | | Chris Sale | 20.1 |
| Jon Niese | 19.2 | | Yordano Ventura | 20.1 |
| Dan Haren | 19.7 | | Jordan Zimmermann | 20.4 |

# THE MISERY INDEX
(Pitcher's BABIP –30%) + (70% - Pitcher's Strand Rate)

During his 1980 Presidential campaign against Jimmy Carter, Ronald Reagan introduced a relatively unknown term into the nation's lexicon. The "Misery Index" combined the rate of inflation with the unemployment rate, and showed with just one number how poorly the economy was doing under Carter.

Years later, the Misery Index has worked its way into baseball as well. Baseball players, in particular pitchers, put up numbers that vary widely from game to game. A Clay Buchholz may one day give up 11 runs in five innings of work, but does that mean he's awful? Or could it mean a visit to the doctor might be on the horizon? A handicapper must look at individual performances and decide if the outing was simply bad luck or a sign of deeper troubles for the pitcher.

The Misery Index is one key method to answer that question. Like Reagan's, this Misery Index uses only two stats to determine how much luck has influenced a pitcher's ERA.

The first statistic is the BABIP. The BABIP tells a handicapper what percentage of balls hit into the field of play become base hits. The league rate is 30%; if a pitcher's BABIP is higher, he has run into some bad luck. If it is lower, the pitcher has caught some breaks along the way.

The Strand Rate is the second piece of the puzzle. The Strand Rate describes how many runners a pitcher leaves on base. The average is 70%. A lower number means bad luck and/or bad bullpen. A higher number indicates the opposite.

A negative number means the pitcher has been lucky. A positive number shows the pitcher has run into bad luck and is pitching better than his numbers indicate. This statistic, concocted by John Burnson, isn't designed to tell a handicapper the quality of a pitcher. Some pitchers are so hittable that it isn't feasible to compare his performance with that of a major league pitcher. The charts below shows you which pitchers had the worst and best luck on the pitching mound in 2014:

## Worst Luck

| | | | |
|---|---|---|---|
| Zach McAllister | 12.0% | Tyler Skaggs | 5.0% |
| Clay Buchholz | 10.0% | Justin Verlander | 5.0% |
| Ricky Nolasco | 8.0% | Brett Oberholtzer | 5.0% |
| Brandon Workman | 6.0% | Kyle Gibson | 4.0% |
| Josh Tomlin, Josh | 6.0% | Drew Hutchison | 4.0% |
| Colby Lewis, Colby | 6.0% | Phil Hughes | 4.0% |

## Best Luck

| | | | |
|---|---|---|---|
| Danny Duffy | -16.0% | Collin McHugh | -10.0% |
| Miguel Pineda | -16.0% | Jon Lester | -10.0% |
| Miguel Gonzalez | -14.0% | Drew Smyly | -9.0% |
| Felix Hernandez | -13.0% | Sonny Gray | -8.0% |
| Chris Young | -12.0% | Chris Tillman | -8.0% |
| Chris Sale, Chris | -12.0% | Masahiro Tanaka | -8.0% |

*"It amazes me how people are often more willing to act based on little or no data than to use data that is a challenge to assemble." — Robert J. Shiller*

# Pitcher Wins

The win is dead. No one cares about this stat anymore, for good reason. It tells us little about the quality of a pitcher. There are five steps leading to a pitcher earning a win:

1) His offense must score runs.
2) He must pitch well enough and not allow too many runs
3) He must last five innings
4) His defense must perform well
5) His bullpen must hold the lead given to them.

A pitcher has no direct control over four of those five steps. Yes, there is a positive correlation between how good a pitcher is and how many wins he has. However, there are so many better indicators of a pitcher's performance that there's just no need to be looking at wins as a way to determine the quality of a pitcher.

There is a hidden benefit to this stat, however. Whenever one hears an announcer or TV personality talk up a pitcher's win total, feel justified in discounting what else that announcer has to say. It is most likely junk.

# PITCHING INJURIES

It isn't easy finding out about injuries. Players often hide them, worried about being Wally Pipp-ed out of the lineup. HIPAA laws restrict the amount of information that can be released to the media. Teams order their doctors and trainers to keep away from the media, further limiting the amount of information available to fans (and gamblers).

In the early '70s, the workloads of pitchers were at historic highs, not counting the Dead Ball era and before. By 1980, the change from a four-man to a five-man rotation was well underway. Pitchers began to be limited in the number of pitches thrown in a game, and relievers were used earlier and earlier in the game. All in the name of protecting the valuable commodity known as the starting pitcher.

However, pitching injuries are at an all-time high. Over 25 major league pitchers either had Tommy John surgery last year or were recovering from the surgery. Jose Fernandez, Casey Kelly, Matt Moore, and Jarrod Parker all went under the knife. The Braves had three go down: Brandon Beachy, Kris Medlen, and Jonny Venters were lost to Tommy John surgery.

There isn't a good explanation for the increase in injuries. Some are blaming the increase in velocity from pitchers. In 2003, Billy Wagner was the only pitcher to throw 25 pitches over 100 mph. Last year, there were eight. If that is what is causing the problems, then the solution won't be easy. Trading a loss in effectiveness for a decreased chance of injury is not a trade most players are willing to make.

Throwing a baseball is an unnatural act. The harder you throw, the harder it is on your arm. Injuries continue to rise despite the greater focus on injury prevention. It's not the training staff's fault. It's not the organization's fault. It's not the player's fault. It's the nature of baseball right now.

There are some rules of thumbs to use when concerned about injuries. The first is to make sure you know a pitcher's injury history. Staying healthy is a skill. If a pitcher has had a series of injuries over the years, chances are he suddenly isn't going to find perfect health. Keep a sharper eye on these types of pitchers. A pitcher coming off an injury the previous season will be more likely to suffer another injury this season.

Another concern for bettors is the possibility of a pitcher hiding an injury. Some pitchers take a lot of pride in not missing starts. Daisuke Matsuzaka kept quiet a leg injury suffered in spring training, forcing him to change his mechanics and causing shoulder problems in 2009. "I didn't want them to think I was making excuses," he explained.

There are four major causes of arm injuries for pitchers:

1. Bad mechanics: if your throwing technique is poor, the likelihood of an injury is much higher. Guys like Adam Wainwright, Chris Sale, and Stephen Strasburg can be dominant over a period of time, but the risk of injury is always high due to the way they throw the ball. David Price and Felix Hernandez have superb mechanics and should continue to be workhorses in the future.

2. Poor conditioning: a pitcher uses his whole body when throwing the ball at top velocity. It isn't just the arm that needs built up. A pitcher's upper legs and lower torso are the most important part of his throwing motion. If these lack strength, problems may arise.

3. Overload: this occurs when a pitcher throws too many stressful pitches in one game. A pitcher who gets into trouble is forced to throw a lot of high-effort pitches in order to get out of the inning. That overload isn't good for his arm.

4. Overuse: when a pitcher throws too often and doesn't have enough time between starts to recover. Managers have become extremely cautious about overusing a starting pitcher, from limiting his pitch count to moving to a five-man rotation. As a

result, overuse rarely comes into play for starters. Relievers are another story, however.

## How to detect arm problems:

- The pitcher starts taking more time between pitches on the mound.
- The pitcher's arm slot is "lower" than normal.
- The pitcher flinches when he releases a pitch.
- The pitcher skips out on his throwing sessions between starts.
- The pitcher doesn't extend his arm all the way on his follow through.
- The pitcher won't throw all the pitches in his arsenal.
- The pitcher "rushes his motion", trying to get more power with his pitches.

Pitching coaches will be able to recognize the warning signs much faster than a guy watching the game on TV. However, pitchers are expected to throw when they are tired. A sore arm is not a surprise, and most pitchers will try to work through it. Sore does not equal hurt. A 90% Clayton Kershaw is still better than long reliever waiting to make a spot start. The key is to find out when Kershaw is only 90%, and get a good price betting against him in that spot.

# COMING OFF THE DL

Few things are more dangerous than betting on a pitcher coming off the disabled list. Especially dangerous is betting on pitchers who don't do a rehab stint in the minor leagues. One quick rule of thumb; don't do it. Everything has a price, however, and sometimes a bettor might find a team undervalued despite starting a questionable pitcher.

One has to make sure the pitcher is healthy. You will often see a pitcher make a start or two and immediately go back on the disabled list. Teams don't start a guy with the knowledge he is going to immediately re-injure himself, but they often don't know what to expect from the pitcher.

You should also know the reason the pitcher went on the disabled list. An arm injury is a red flag. A leg injury, not so much. Pitchers often come back too quickly from an injury and struggle. They can also be rusty; the longer the time on the DL, the rustier they will be. If a pitcher hasn't been on the disabled list long, you can reasonably project how well that pitcher will perform.

There is no one-size-fits-all strategy for dealing with pitching injuries, however. A pitcher's skill set, the type of his injury, rehab reports, and whom he will face will all come into play. A pitcher who misses just two starts, is inserted back into the rotation after the 15 day minimum, and pitching at home against the Mets is probably a safe play. One who has been out for a month and in line to start at Coors is probably someone to avoid.

*You should always stay hungry. Stay hungry, so you can eat. – Syed Balkhi*

# DEALING WITH BULLPENS

Bullpens are the Russian roulette of baseball betting. A handicapper can reasonably estimate how well a team will hit, and how well the starting pitcher will throw. But not so much with the bullpen. A bettor doesn't know who will be pitching, when he will be pitching, or whom that pitcher will be throwing against.

It isn't just gamblers who have problems with the bullpen. Managers are hired and fired based on their abilities to handle the bullpen. Opinions vary widely on just how to use a closer, middle reliever, left-handed specialist, and so on. Simply put, it is tricky for both experts in the game and bettors to predict what the bullpen performance will be from game to game.

On top of that, the randomness of relief pitching makes it difficult to trust the numbers put up by a bullpen. A pitcher doesn't throw enough innings to make the numbers very credible. But that is what we are left with, so we have to make the best of it.

There are three numbers that I start with to determine the overall strength of a bullpen:

- Cumulative ERA: This is simply the ERA of the team's bullpen. Everything counts, from the first inning numbers when a starter is knocked out to the extra-inning games.
- ERA from the 7th inning on: This stat counts starters who go deep into the game. It eliminates the innings where a starting pitcher is pulled early and the long reliever throws.
- Late and close: tells me how strong the key members of the bullpen are. The typical pitchers in these games are the main setup man and the closer.

The main reason I use these three numbers is that they are available on various websites and are simple to download into a spreadsheet.

These are just the base rates I use to start estimating my bullpen power numbers for a particular game, however. More work needs to be done.

Each team generally carries seven relief pitchers: One closer, a couple of set-up men, one or two left-handed specialists, and one or two long relievers/emergency starter types. When Clayton Kershaw is on the mound, you can automatically discard all but two relievers. If Kershaw is roughed up, chances are the bet is lost regardless of how well the long relievers pitch. Since he will usually go deep into a game and hand the ball over with the lead (or just finish it himself), I will only care about which relievers finish the 8th and 9th innings. In his case, I'll give much far more weight to the "Late and Close" ERA of a team.

If Hyun-Jin Ryu is starting for the Dodgers instead of Kershaw, I will lower the bullpen rating a significant amount. Ryu, an effective pitcher, still won't go deep into games and will force the middle relievers to carry some of the load in the game. Rather than having the closer finish out the game, we have to hope the middle part of the pen can keep the Dodgers in the ball game. In this case, I may put more emphasis on the overall rating of a bullpen rather than focus on the "late and close" numbers.

One also has to take into account how well rested a team's bullpen is. If a closer has thrown three straight days, he won't be on the mound that day. If the setup man went two innings the day before, he may only be available for one inning. Daily charts regarding bullpen use are necessary. A team's power rating for the bullpen can swing up or down dramatically depending on who is available. One also must account for the Rule of 17, a Tom Tango creation that states a relief pitcher gets 17% more K, allows 17% fewer HR, allows 17 points fewer in BABIP, and 17% fewer runs. Relievers naturally have a better ERA than starters and a bettor has to make adjustments based on that fact.

There are no simple ways to judge a bullpen. A bettor has to be flexible, pay close attention to the use of a team's pitchers, and hope for the best. If done correctly, a bettor will find proper bullpen ratings to be one of the more profitable angles in baseball.

# CREATING THE LINE

When making your own baseball line, it is important to remember the old adage "Garbage in, Garbage out". If you use junk stats, you will end up with a junk number that is as good as flipping a coin to make your picks. Accurate power numbers on offense, defense, and pitching are all needed to make a true, reliable line.

# PYTHAGOREAN FORMULA

There are a number of formulas that can be used to create a baseball line. The most common formula used is called the Pythagorean Theory. Bill James created Pythagorean; he used it to confirm his belief that the true measure of a team was its ratio between runs scored and runs allowed. James's initial formula was to square the total number of runs scored, then divide that number by the square of the number of runs allowed plus the square of the number of runs scored.

WIN %  = (RUNS FOR ^2)/((RUNS ALLOWED^2)+(RUNS FOR^2))

In Excel, the formula is written down as:

= (POWER (A1, 2))/((POWER (A1, 2)+(POWER (B1, 2))))

Runs Scored equals A1, and Runs Allowed equals B1.

James later tweaked this formula slightly to make it even more accurate: instead of using two as the exponent, he used 1.83.

WIN %  = (RUNS^1.83)/((RUNS ALLOWED^1.83)+(RUNS ^1.83))

In a typical game, this was an extremely accurate barometer. In games where the run environment was higher (Texas) or lower (San Diego), however, the accuracy suffered.

# THE DAVENPORT SOLUTION

Clay Davenport effectively solved this problem. His formula was similar to James:

> Win % = (Runs ^Exponent) / ((Runs allowed^Exponent)+(Runs^Exponent))

The unique part of his method was the use of changing exponents to adapt to the run-scoring environment. Davenport first determined the run-scoring environment using this adjustment:

> 1.5 * log (expected runs per game for both teams) +. 45

In Excel, Davenport's calculation is expressed as:

> = 1.5*LOG (A1) + 0.45

A1 equals the total amount of runs expected for both teams.

This formula gives us different exponents depending on the run environment:

| RUNS/ GAME | EXP | RUNS / GAME | EXP |
|:---:|:---:|:---:|:---:|
| 1 | 0.450 | 9 | 1.881 |
| 2 | 0.902 | 10 | 1.950 |
| 3 | 1.166 | 11 | 2.012 |
| 4 | 1.353 | 12 | 2.069 |
| 5 | 1.498 | 13 | 2.121 |
| 6 | 1.617 | 14 | 2.169 |
| 7 | 1.718 | 15 | 2.214 |

Where James used just one number as the exponent, Davenport was able to adjust from game to game. It fixes the key flaw in formulas similar to James. In these cases, a team winning each game 6-3 will have an equal winning percentage as the team that typically wins each game 2-

1. Since the Runs Scored/Runs Allowed ratio is the same, the winning percentage is the same.

Theoretically, this may make sense; reality dismisses such a belief. An outmatched basketball team will often slow down the tempo to shorten the game; the fewer possessions, the fewer chances for the better team to exploit its edge in talent. The same holds true in baseball. The lower amount of scoring, the more likely one fortunate play will determine the winner of the game.

In a typical run environment, a team expected to win 6-3 would have a 79% chance of winning the game. It is in the extreme run environments that Davenport's method makes its impact.

Using Davenport's method (written in Excel) you will see different winning percentages depending on the run environment:

| Runs | Opp run | Tot Runs | Exponent |
|------|---------|----------|----------|
| 8 | 4 | 12 | 2.07 |
| 6 | 3 | 9 | 1.88 |
| 4 | 2 | 6 | 1.62 |
| 2 | 1 | 3 | 1.17 |

The variables above are translated into an expected winning percentage by using the following formula in Excel:

| Formula in Excel | W % | Line |
|------------------|-----|------|
| =Power(8,2.07) / ((Power(8,2.07)+(Power(4,2.07)))) | 81% | -4.20 |
| =Power(6,1.88) / ((Power(6,1.88)+(Power(3,1.88)))) | 79% | -3.68 |
| =Power(4,1.62) / ((Power(4,1.62)+(Power(2,1.62)))) | 75% | -3.07 |
| =Power(2,1.17) / ((Power(2,1.17)+(Power(1,1.17)))) | 69% | -2.24 |

As a matter of practice, I prefer using the sportsbooks Over/Under line to determine what exponent I use in Davenport's formula. The next page lists the exponents depending on the listed line:

| Total | Exponent | | Total | Exponent |
|-------|----------|---|-------|----------|
| 6.5 | 1.67 | | 10 | 1.95 |
| 7 | 1.72 | | 10.5 | 1.98 |
| 7.5 | 1.76 | | 11 | 2.01 |
| 8 | 1.8 | | 11.5 | 2.04 |
| 8.5 | 1.84 | | 12 | 2.07 |
| 9 | 1.88 | | 12.5 | 2.1 |
| 9.5 | 1.92 | | 13 | 2.12 |

## PYTHAGENPAT

Another winning percentage estimator was developed by David Smith. It also uses a floating exponent that changes depending on the runs per game. The formula is a bit simpler than the Davenport solution:

EXPONENT= RUNS PER GAME ^ .287

> **WINNING %= RUNS ^ EXPONENT /**
> **(RUNS ^ EXPONENT) + (RUNS ALLOWED ^ EXPONENT)**

*I have not failed. I've just found 10,000 ways that won't work. – Thomas Edison*

*Do not wait to strike until the iron is hot; but make it hot by striking. – William B. Sprague*

# BUILDING THE MODEL

So how does it all work? Let's use the September 28, 2007 game between the Florida Marlins and New York Mets. The Mets were in the midst of a historical collapse. With just seventeen games to go, New York had been a comfortable seven games in first place. A 4-10 stretch left the Mets tied with Philadelphia going into the final weekend of the season. Oliver Perez was on the mound for the Mets, facing Byung Hyun Kim of the Marlins. Florida, despite being on a four game winning streak, was 18 games behind the Mets and the Phillies in the division and suffering through a season from hell. New York was -200 favorite. The process below will detail just one method in creating your own line on a baseball game.

## STEP 1: ESTIMATING EACH TEAM'S OFFENSE

The Florida Marlins on base average for the season is .337. Its slugging average was .450. Multiplying those two numbers will give me a .1516 OTS number. The average National League team has an on base average of .334 and a .423 slugging average. The league average OTS is .1413. Dividing the Marlins OTS number by the league average OTS will give me a 1.07 number; this means the Florida Marlins overall offense is 7% above league average.

The Marlins overall OTS number is just the starting point. I need to make possible adjustments. The Mets starter is a lefty; I want to see how well Florida hits lefties. Against left-handers, the Marlins splits are .345/.451. Those numbers average out to be about 10% above league average. The 3% difference seems significant, but it really isn't. Oliver Perez will be on a short hook tonight and may or may not reach the sixth inning. So while the Marlins hit lefties better than righties, the knowledge that the lefty may not be long for the game means I have to be careful when adjusting my power ratings based on the arm of the opposing pitcher.

There are other variables that I look at when making my offensive power ratings for a game. Home/away splits are important in some cases. How well a team has been hitting is relevant in others. Injuries, or players getting rest, matter at times also. In the case of this game, however, my concerns are limited. Florida has an offense about 8% above league average.

I go through the same process with the Mets. New York's batting splits are .342/.431; its OTS is .1474 compared to the .1412 league average. After dividing those two numbers, I get New York's basic offensive power rating is 1.04. A right-hander is on the mound for Florida; New York has hit about 9% higher than league average against righties on the season. Byung-Hyun Kim is also one of those pitchers that have huge platoon splits. These two splits mean I need to increase the Mets' power rating. Shea Stadium plays a role as well, decreasing run scoring by about 5% over the course of the season. Taking these additional factors into consideration, I make New York's offensive power rating about a 1.10. The Marlins' offensive rating is 1.08.

## STEP 2: ESTIMATING THE PITCHING

Kim was one of the worst pitchers in the National League in the 2007 season. Starting the season with the Colorado Rockies, Kim also saw time with the Marlins and the Arizona. He moved into the starting rotation for Florida in September and had been rocked in his previous five starts. I looked at a variety of numbers to help me determine how well Kim was expected to throw.

- Season ERA: 6.09
- September ERA: 7.50
- xERA: 5.42
- FIP ERA: 5.41

Kim had been striking out batters at the league average rate, but couldn't consistently throw strikes and was getting lit up because of it. Using the above information, I expected Kim to have a 5.70 ERA in about five innings of work. Against a league average offense, Kim would allow 3.17 runs in those five innings of work.

The other four innings of work was going to be thrown by the Marlins bullpen. Florida's pen had struggled at times, and I made its power rating for the bullpen at about 8% worse than average. Since the average ERA in the National League is 4.43, Florida's bullpen ERA is given a 4.78 rating. They will allow 2.13 runs in the final four innings of the game. All told, the Marlins pitching would allow 5.30 runs versus a league average offense. If I divide 5.3 runs by 4.43 (average NL ERA), I get a pitching power rating of 1.20 for the Marlins. Florida's pitching performance will theoretically be 20% worse than the league average.

I now do the same for the Mets. Oliver Perez has these numbers:

- Season ERA: 3.56
- September ERA: 2.88
- xERA: 3.94
- FIP ERA: 3.32

Perez's September ERA was helped by the fact he allowed six unearned runs that month. He had been throwing OK but wasn't dominating like his FIP ERA and September ERA indicate. I gave him a rating of 4.00 ERA in seven innings pitched. Against a league average team, Perez would be expected to allow 3.1 runs in seven innings of work.

New York's bullpen would carry the load the final two innings. The Mets raw numbers indicate a powerful bullpen. It wasn't at the time. The pen was exhausted and a key factor of its late season collapse. I judge New York's bullpen at slightly below average. I don't use that number, however. Since Perez is expected to go seven innings, a rested Aaron Heilman and Billy Wagner should close out the game. Those two are high quality pitchers, and I give the Mets pen a rating about 5% better than average. They will allow .93 runs over the final two innings. For the game, the Marlins would be expected to score 4.03 runs in this game. I divide that number by 4.43 (average NL ERA) to get a 91% power rating.

## STEP 3: EXPECTED RUNS SCORED

To determine the number of runs a team can expect to score, multiply the team's offensive power rating by its opponent's pitching rating, then multiply that number by the average runs scored in the league.

Florida Offense rating (1.08) * Mets Pitching rating (.91) * 4.71
Florida is expected to score 4.63 runs in an average ballpark.

Mets offense rating (1.10) * Florida Pitching rating (1.20) * 4.71
New York should score 6.22 runs in a league average park.

## STEP 4: DETERMINE EXPECTED WINNING PERCENTAGE

The Total is set at 9.5, meaning the exponent in the Davenport Solution is 1.916. The formula in Excel will look like this:

=Power (6.22, 1.916) / ((Power (4.63, 1.916) + (Power (6.22, 1.916))

New York's expected winning percentage, before home field advantage is considered, is 64% for a true line of -1.76. Florida's line would be the opposite: they would be priced at 1.76.

## STEP 5: HOME FIELD ADVANTAGE ADJUSTMENTS

The Mets collapse had mostly taken place at Shea Stadium; New York was riding a seven game home losing streak coming into the September 28 game. The late season pressure was getting to the Mets, and playing at home obviously was making matters worse. In May, I had given New York sixteen cents on the money line in a series between these two same teams. I couldn't do that for this series. There was no home field advantage. In fact, I could make a good argument that I needed to adjust the Mets down for playing at home. My price: Mets -1.76.

Now the handicapping really begins. Have the Mets regrouped after blowing a division lead that they held for five months? Does Florida care about the game, or are they going through the motions at the end of the season? Is Florida going to play its key players? How overworked is the Marlins bullpen? Many variables need to be examined before betting the game. Creating your own line only indicates possible plays. Don't make it out to be any more than that. All these intangibles, and the nice price, pointed towards Florida in this game.

So how did the game end up? Kim gave up four runs in five innings. The Marlins bullpen was surprisingly effective: four relievers shut out the Mets and allowed just four hits. The Mets pen was strong as well, allowing only one run in over five innings of work. The problem for New York was its starter. Oliver Perez didn't make it out of the fourth inning, getting hammered for six runs and dropping the Mets out its first place tie with Philadelphia. Florida 7, New York 4. For all intents and purposes, the Mets' season was over.

*"Investors should be skeptical of history-based models. Constructed by a nerdy-sounding priesthood using esoteric terms such as beta, gamma, sigma and the like, these models tend to look impressive. Too often, though, investors forget to examine the assumptions behind the models. Beware of geeks bearing formulas."*
*Warren Buffett*

# THE PHYSICS OF BASEBALL

The role of physics and the environment is rarely mentioned in baseball, but it can be a major factor when betting a game. Some effects are obvious, such as the increased scoring at Coors Field or the lowered run totals when the wind is blowing in. However, other effects are a bit more subtle. Game-time temperature, barometric pressure, and humidity all are possible influences on an individual baseball game. Dr. Robert Adair, Professor of Physics at Yale, was asked by Commissioner Bart Giamatti to study the elements of baseball that are affected by physics. The book that followed Adair's research is both a fascinating read and a valuable resource in handicapping, particularly when you play totals.

### Altitude

Altitude is the prime reason why Coors Field is so brutal to pitchers. The more you rise above sea level, the less dense air is. Air density plays a key factor in determining how far a batted ball travels, how fast it travels, and how much it moves when it travels.

These reasons conspire to make Coors a hitter's paradise. A curve ball that might drop eight inches more (in comparison to a fastball) will drop only four inches because of the thin air. It also will break less because it crosses home plate faster; the ball doesn't have time to break the way it would at sea level. A fastball is six inches quicker in Coors than at Shea Stadium. That may be good for a pitcher in theory, but the batter will gladly trade a slightly faster pitch for less movement.

The defense suffers as well from the low density. Outfielders, already having problems handling the vast expanse of the Rockies outfield, discovered that balls hit into the gap at Coors fly further and land quicker. This costs a typical outfielder eight to nine feet in range. An infielder also loses range. Adair estimates that a shortstop loses about a foot in range because of the low air density, a significant amount in this game of inches.

Coors is the best known for altitude effects, but many other stadiums in baseball are impacted as well. These parks obviously don't have the elevation of Coors, but they still show considerable differences when compared to `sea-level' parks.

Adair estimates that a ball hit 400 feet in San Francisco would travel an additional seven feet every 1000 feet in elevation. The same ball hit in Pittsburgh would fly about 408 feet. In Atlanta, the ball would go about 407 feet. In Detroit, it would travel 404 feet. Altitude matters. The chart below shows the impact on a 400-foot fly ball for each stadium.

| TEAM | ALTITUDE | DIST | TEAM | ALT | DIST |
|---|---|---|---|---|---|
| Anaheim | 160 | 401 | Milwaukee | 635 | 404 |
| Arizona | 1090 | 408 | Minnesota | 815 | 406 |
| Atlanta | 1050 | 407 | Yankees | 55 | 400 |
| Baltimore | 20 | 400 | Mets | 55 | 400 |
| Boston | 21 | 400 | Oakland | 25 | 400 |
| Chi Cubs | 595 | 404 | Philly | 5 | 400 |
| White Sox | 595 | 404 | Pittsburgh | 730 | 405 |
| Cincinnati | 550 | 404 | San Diego | 13 | 400 |
| Cleveland | 777 | 405 | Seattle | 400 | 403 |
| Colorado | 5280 | 437 | San Fran | 75 | 401 |
| Detroit | 633 | 404 | St Louis | 455 | 403 |
| Florida | 10 | 400 | Tampa Bay | 15 | 400 |
| Houston | 22 | 400 | Texas | 551 | 404 |
| Kansas City | 750 | 405 | Toronto | 300 | 402 |
| Los Angeles | 340 | 402 | Washington | 25 | 400 |

**Ball Temperature**

The temperature of game ball affects the game as well. Softball players have been known to put game balls in the microwave before playing a game; how long this nuked ball stays hot is hard to tell but the theory behind the action is correct. Each 10-degree increase in ball temperature will result in the 400-foot fly ball traveling an additional four feet. Warning track power on a normal ball may be a home run with a ball 10 degrees hotter.

Old timers tell stories about John McGraw storing balls in an icebox, to be used only when the visiting team is at the plate. This might have worked years ago, but MLB has since changed the rules and dictated that all balls used in the game must be supplied to the umpires two hours before game time.

## Game Time Temperature

The hotter the day, the farther the ball goes. If it is hot outside, the ball temperature naturally tends to rise as well. Air density is also reduced. For each 10-degree rise in heat, the 400-foot drive hit at sea level would go four feet further. Hot days lead to more runs. As a rule of thumb, add ½ run to your own total number if the game time temperature is over 90 degrees. If it is below 55 degrees, subtract ½ run from your total.

However, don't go overboard if the weather is cold. Pitches break less in cold weather, forcing pitchers to start off-speed pitches on a different trajectory. Cold weather favors a power pitcher over a finesse pitcher who relies on location to succeed.

Pay close attention to the home plate umpire as well. More than a few will widen the strike zone if they don't like the weather.

## Barometer

When barometric pressure is lower, so is the air resistance to a ball in flight. Each 1-inch drop in barometric pressure results in a six-foot increase in the length of a 400-foot fly ball.

# Humidity

The heavier the ball, the less distance it will travel. A ball stored at 100% humidity for four weeks will weigh 11% more than a typical ball. The 'bounce' of the ball is also affected. The humidity ball will travel 30 feet less than a ball stored at low humidity. This effect may have merit at Coors, which began storing their balls in a humidifier in 2003. For the most part, however, the game time humidity has little bearing on the number of runs scored in a game. Jan Null, director of meteorology for Planetweather.com, says this about humidity and its effect on a baseball:

"The air is approximately 21 percent oxygen, 78 percent nitrogen and some very small amounts of other gases. Now if we look at the weight of the molecules (i.e., molecular weight) of dry air we see it has a value of 29. But gaseous water vapor has a molecular weight of only 18. Because the air around us is a mixture of dry air and water vapor, its actual molecular weight falls somewhere between 18 and 29, with it being less on humid days. When the air becomes more humid, its density lessens, so it creates less drag or friction, which would slow a baseball or allow it to curve.

However, the dynamics aren't quite that simple because high humidity can cause a baseball to gain a small amount of water, which makes it slightly heavier. The bottom line is that the effect of humidity, all other things being equal, is negligible."

# Wind

The first thing a better does each morning is to check the weather report at Wrigley Field. Wind blowing in off the lake means a low total; wind blowing out means the opposite. Each one-mph increase in wind adds three feet to a 400-foot drive. However, that is a bit misleading. A 400-foot drive with 20-mph wind blowing out to left field won't go 460 feet. All stadiums have grandstands acting as wind blocks; the 20-mph wind to center field may only be five mph around home plate. Once the ball gets up in the air, the wind will take over. Nevertheless, generally, most batted balls aren't as affected as they would be if the wind were blowing in.

A hidden effect of the wind may occur to the pitcher as well. Wind doesn't affect fastballs; the average fastball traveling 90 mph crosses home plate .4 seconds after the ball is released. If a 10-mph wind is blowing in the pitcher's face, that 90 mph pitch will only slow down to 89 mph.

However, wind creates havoc with off-speed pitches. In the case of crosswinds, a curve ball may break as many as 21 inches or as few as 8 inches. Gusty days can plays havoc on pitchers who must locate their off-speed pitches. Pay close attention to wind speed when a finesse pitcher is on the mound.

Defense is also affected by wind. Wind-blown pop-ups and fly balls often fall between defensive players, resulting in an unfair hit being charged to the pitcher. Some stadiums are effective in blocking wind. Others just make it swirl, causing havoc for everyone involved. The numbers below show the effects of heavy wind in comparison to extremely slight/still wind.

| WIND SPEED | Gms | ERRORS/Gm | RUNS/GM | BB/GM | K'S/GM |
|---|---|---|---|---|---|
| Over 20 MPH | 290 | 1.52 | 10.8 | 7.37 | 12.83 |
| 2 MPH or less | 234 | 1.47 | 10.4 | 6.73 | 12.39 |

The wind has more of an impact on day games than games in the evening. If the weather sites show heavy winds during the day, don't assume it will keep blowing for a night game. Wind also blows harder in April and May. Once summer hits, the wind doesn't affect nearly as many ballgames as it they did early in the season. Below are the wind charts for cities with outdoor stadiums. This likely goes into the "too much information" category, but here it is nonetheless.

| TEAM | April | May | June | July | Aug | Sept | Oct |
|---|---|---|---|---|---|---|---|
| Arizona | 6.9 | 7 | 6.7 | 7.1 | 6.6 | 6.3 | 5.8 |
| Atlanta | 10.1 | 8.7 | 8.1 | 7.7 | 7.3 | 8 | 8.5 |
| Baltimore | 10.2 | 8.9 | 8.2 | 7.6 | 7.5 | 7.7 | 8.1 |
| Boston | 13.1 | 12 | 11.4 | 11 | 10.8 | 11.3 | 11.9 |
| Chicago | 11.9 | 10.5 | 9.3 | 8.4 | 8.2 | 8.9 | 10.1 |
| Cincinnati | 10.6 | 8.7 | 7.9 | 7.2 | 6.8 | 7.4 | 8.1 |
| Cleveland | 11.5 | 10 | 9.2 | 8.6 | 8.2 | 8.9 | 9.9 |
| Colorado | 10 | 9.3 | 8.8 | 8.3 | 8 | 7.9 | 7.8 |
| Detroit | 11.3 | 10.1 | 9.2 | 8.5 | 8.1 | 8.7 | 9.7 |
| Florida | 10.5 | 9.5 | 8.3 | 7.9 | 7.9 | 8.2 | 9.2 |
| Kansas City | 12.3 | 10.3 | 9.9 | 9.2 | 8.8 | 9.6 | 10.5 |
| Los Angeles | 8.5 | 8.4 | 8 | 7.9 | 7.7 | 7.3 | 6.9 |
| Milwaukee | 12.8 | 11.5 | 10.4 | 9.7 | 9.5 | 10.4 | 11.4 |
| New York | 12.9 | 11.6 | 11 | 10.4 | 10.3 | 11 | 11.6 |
| Philadelphia | 10.8 | 9.5 | 8.8 | 8.2 | 8 | 8.3 | 8.8 |
| Pittsburgh | 10.2 | 8.7 | 8 | 7.3 | 6.8 | 7.4 | 8.3 |
| San Diego | 7.8 | 7.9 | 7.8 | 7.5 | 7.4 | 7.1 | 6.5 |
| San Francisco | 12.2 | 13.4 | 14 | 13.6 | 12.8 | 11.1 | 9.4 |
| St. Louis | 11.3 | 9.4 | 8.8 | 8 | 7.6 | 8.2 | 8.9 |
| Texas | 12.4 | 11.1 | 10.6 | 9.8 | 8.9 | 9.3 | 9.7 |

# MONTH BY MONTH SCORING

Scoring isn't lower early in the season because the hitters are behind the pitchers coming out of spring training. The cold weather keeps the run scoring down compared to the summer months. As the weather warms up, so does the scoring. Each park can play differently at different times of the year, however.

## Arizona, Atlanta, and Baltimore

Run scoring dips when the roof is closed in **Arizona,** leading to a drop in runs once summer kicks into gear. Over in night games, Under during the day. **Atlanta's** park plays normal for the summer months but scoring is lower than average in April and September. Lower scoring at night. **Baltimore** has a surge in August; however, that could be fluky based on the rest of the season.

## Boston, the Cubs, and the White Sox

The **Red Sox** scoring takes a spike in August; weather most likely gets the credit. The **Cubs** scoring fluctuates all season, usually depending on the direction of the wind. As the weather heats up, so does scoring in the **White Sox's** home park. The home run rate increases dramatically as the season turns into summer.

## Cincinnati, Cleveland, and Colorado

Scoring in **Cincinnati** starts off strong, and then gradually gets lower as the season wears on. The **Indians** likewise sees more runs scored in the first part of the season. Day games seem to go Under, while night games lean Over. **Colorado** does have some weather problems early and late in the season, but they do not seem to affect scoring on a macro level.

## Detroit, Florida, and Houston

**Detroit** plays at league average for most of the season, with the exception being April. The bats start out quick in **Houston**, but scoring takes a dive as the season gets going and stays there the rest of the way. Air conditioning probably deserves most of the blame. The **Royals** scoring seems to follow along with the weather: the hotter it is, the more runs scored. Wind may play a big role as well.

## LAA Angels, Los Angeles, Miami, and Milwaukee

Run scoring in **Anaheim** peaks in July and August before dropping to a new low in September **Los Angeles** remains steady, other than a short blip in June. Other factors probably come into play. **Miami** has a newer park and not a big sample, so it is too early to get a read on how it plays. **Milwaukee** doesn't deal with cold or otherwise bad weather. If it is uncomfortable outside, the roof will close.

## Minnesota, the Yankees, and the Mets

The **Twins** play outdoors up north, so weather will have a huge factor in how the park plays. Under during the day, Over at night. The same situation applies with the **Yankees** and **Mets**; wind and cold weather will play a large role.

## Oakland, Philadelphia, and Pittsburgh

**Oakland** plays one way during the day, and one way during the night. Wind is also a major factor. **Philadelphia** peaks in August; temperature plays. **Pittsburgh** is the opposite, peaking in August while bottoming out in June. I don't take much stock into either of those fluctuations.

## San Diego, Seattle, and San Francisco

The **Padres'** ballpark looks steady other than a summer bump. Day games means more runs. **Seattle** is steady as well, most likely due to its roof that will keep bad weather out. The increase in July and August might be due to the roof being open more often. The **Giants'** location next to the bay means factors other than game time temperature play a bigger role in scoring.

## St. Louis, Tampa Bay, Texas

The **Cardinals** see an increase in runs during the summer, but that dips back down as the weather cools. **Tampa** plays every home game inside, so any change in the scoring rate is due to something other than weather. **Texas** plays in one of the highest scoring parks in the country, due in no small part because of the temperature and wind effects. Pay particular attention to the wind. Day games lean towards the Under.

## Toronto and Washington

The **Blue Jays** close the roof when the weather is poor, so fluctuations in scoring aren't from the weather. Under during the day, Over at night. **Washington** sees low scoring in April then rebounds towards its average the rest of the season. Under seems to be the trend during day games.

# Monthly Runs Per Game for Each Ballpark

| Team | Overall | Apr | May | Jun | Jul | Aug | Sep |
|------|---------|-----|-----|-----|-----|-----|-----|
| Arizona | 9.37 | 9.91 | 9.71 | 9.30 | 9.14 | 9.15 | 8.83 |
| Atlanta | 8.18 | 8.03 | 8.45 | 7.85 | 8.82 | 8.05 | 7.63 |
| Baltimore | 9.62 | 9.06 | 9.56 | 9.44 | 9.60 | 10.37 | 9.81 |
| Boston | 9.89 | 9.97 | 9.69 | 9.52 | 9.62 | 10.28 | 10.12 |
| Cubs | 8.96 | 9.45 | 8.72 | 8.79 | 8.93 | 9.02 | 9.01 |
| White Sox | 9.25 | 8.63 | 8.54 | 9.46 | 9.39 | 9.94 | 9.42 |
| Cincinnati | 8.88 | 9.50 | 9.64 | 8.77 | 8.42 | 8.91 | 7.98 |
| Cleveland | 8.96 | 9.45 | 9.01 | 9.35 | 8.50 | 8.61 | 8.79 |
| Colorado | 10.82 | 10.67 | 10.32 | 10.84 | 10.88 | 11.24 | 10.92 |
| Detroit | 9.55 | 10.13 | 9.09 | 9.45 | 9.50 | 9.64 | 9.58 |
| Houston | 8.70 | 8.99 | 8.72 | 8.94 | 9.06 | 8.23 | 8.33 |
| Kansas City | 8.97 | 8.93 | 9.17 | 8.95 | 9.43 | 8.71 | 8.90 |
| LA Angels | 8.77 | 8.72 | 8.54 | 8.78 | 9.11 | 9.16 | 8.19 |
| Dodgers | 7.85 | 8.63 | 8.07 | 6.96 | 7.37 | 7.87 | 8.46 |
| Miami | 7.90 | 7.90 | 8.60 | 8.98 | 6.88 | 7.43 | 7.27 |
| Milwaukee | 9.07 | 9.07 | 9.09 | 9.18 | 9.21 | 9.41 | 8.54 |
| Minnesota | 9.09 | 9.60 | 8.52 | 9.11 | 9.30 | 9.01 | 9.18 |
| Mets | 7.85 | 7.81 | 7.61 | 7.93 | 8.65 | 7.67 | 7.69 |
| Yankees | 9.30 | 9.16 | 9.55 | 9.01 | 9.25 | 9.29 | 9.41 |
| Oakland | 8.20 | 8.11 | 7.93 | 7.92 | 8.36 | 7.99 | 8.97 |
| Philly | 8.89 | 9.47 | 8.54 | 8.80 | 9.54 | 8.68 | 8.36 |
| Pittsburgh | 8.41 | 8.04 | 7.74 | 8.12 | 8.56 | 9.36 | 8.72 |
| San Diego | 7.24 | 7.10 | 7.02 | 7.63 | 7.68 | 7.27 | 6.86 |
| San Fran | 7.77 | 7.73 | 8.03 | 6.90 | 7.72 | 8.09 | 8.08 |
| Seattle | 7.73 | 8.14 | 7.42 | 7.32 | 7.56 | 8.50 | 7.34 |
| St. Louis | 8.47 | 8.10 | 8.72 | 8.54 | 8.38 | 8.72 | 8.44 |
| Tampa | 8.34 | 9.00 | 8.56 | 7.96 | 7.82 | 8.00 | 8.64 |
| Texas | 10.03 | 9.96 | 9.96 | 10.56 | 9.72 | 9.90 | 10.02 |
| Toronto | 9.19 | 9.50 | 9.33 | 9.02 | 9.67 | 8.93 | 8.77 |
| Nationals | 8.48 | 7.77 | 8.80 | 7.57 | 8.82 | 8.91 | 9.12 |

# THE STRIKE ZONE

The rulebook defines the strike zone as "that area over home plate which is a horizontal line at the midpoint between the top of the shoulders and the top of the uniform pants, and the lower level is a line at the top of the knees. The strike zone shall be determined from the batter's stance as the batter is prepared to swing."

In theory, the strike zone seems simple. In actuality however, it is a judgment call from the home plate umpire. Each batter's strike zone is different from the next, depending on a batter's position when he is swinging the bat. Jimmy Rollins's strike zone is smaller than Eric Hosmer's because Rollins is A) 5 feet 9 inches tall compared to Hosmer's height of 6 feet 4 inches, and B) Hosmer stands high when he's in the box while Rollins tends to crouch.

This is a discrepancy acknowledged by everyone involved in the game. According to most players, a good umpire is one whose strike zone is consistent from one player's first at-bat to his next. If, however, the high strike is called a ball in the first inning but a strike in the fifth, then the players will have a problem.

Today's strike zone has evolved into an oval more than the rectangle dictated in the rulebooks. The high strike simply isn't called much anymore.

Current Strike Zone          True Strike Zone

Computer technology was brought into baseball when MLB became concerned about length of the game and the inconsistency of the home plate umpire. First Ques-tec, now PitchFx. Both systems use cameras and tracking devices to help determine whether a pitch was called correctly by an umpire. Over the course of a game, an umpire might miss up to a dozen pitches (according to PitchFx). It isn't easy being behind the plate.

A pitcher's umpire will go under; a hitter's umpire will tend to go over. The size of the strike zone is the key. Obviously the more walks in the game the more runs will be scored.

However, walks don't tell the whole story. Assume that the pitcher just threw a 2-1 pitch on the outside corner of the plate. A pitcher's umpire will call that strike two. The hitter's umpire will make the count 3-1. It is impossible to minimize the importance of the 2-1 pitch. American League hitters, with a 2-2 count, had a .271 slugging percentage last season. With a 3-1 count, American League hitters had a .598 slugging percentage. To put that into perspective, the batter with the best slugging percentage in the American League (Jose Abreu) had a .581 slugging percentage. That call on the corner, depending on which way it went, either turned the average hitter into a bad Derek Jeter (.313 slug % in 2014), or a better version of Mike Trout.

An umpire sees hundreds of thousands of pitches throughout his career. He already has his strike zone defined by the time he reaches the major leagues, and as such will tend to keep calling balls and strikes the way he always has. A pitcher's umpire will likely remain one until he retires. The same holds true for a hitter's umpire. A successful gambler must know which is which. He must know what way that 2-1 pitches will likely go. Failure to keep detailed, accurate records will mean failure to maximize your profits over the course of the baseball season.

# CATCHER FRAMING

Turning a borderline pitch into a strike is one of the most important jobs a catcher can do for his pitcher. In the outstanding book The Diamond Appraised, pitcher Tom House discusses how catchers can steal a strike or two.

"No umpire will ever admit this, but of course the catcher influences the ball-strike calls," said House. "And there are some pretty reliable rules for how to do it:

- Receive the ball - don't reach or grab for it. This will make it look as though the pitch is right where you wanted it. No pitch you have to reach for will ever look like a strike, even if it is.

- Move predictably and deliberately; don't jump around.

- Maintain a tempo. Don't let the game drag with constant trips to the mound or by being slow to set up.

- If you question a call, do it with your head still and facing the pitcher. Don't drop your head in frustration, turn around to yell, or hold the ball where you caught it extra-long to prove it was a strike. Umps hate to be shown up, and they'll get even if you do it.

- Frame the strike zone, but don't try to frame obvious balls.

- Catch the low strike with the glove up, and you'll probably get the call; roll the glove over, and you'll lose it."

The advent of PitchFx has brought new attention to the art of catching. It has also allowed us to measure a catcher's impact on the strike zone. Each mistake, a strike call when it should have been a ball or vice versa, is worth .133 run. A catcher who can turn two potential balls into strikes can be extremely valuable to a team even if he can't hit a lick.

The worst catcher in the league, according to data from Baseball Prospectus, was Jarrod Saltalamacchia. He cost his team an average of 2.92 strikes, good for .388 runs per game. That RPG number is around nine cents translated into the money line. Anthony Recker's poor framing skills were worth around seven cents on the money line. However, Kurt Suzuki, Dioner Navarro, and Welington Castillo also hurt their teams due to their bad framing.

The best framing catcher last year was Rene Rivera. The San Diego Padres catcher, a 30-year-old rookie who has toiled mostly in the minors since he was 17, turned 5.42 balls per game into strikes. That was worth an incredible .72 RPG and 19 cents on the money line.

"It comes with time," Rivera said of his pitch-framing expertise. "My first five years of pro ball, (then-Mariners minor league catching coordinator) Roger Hansen worked with me every day, receiving, blocking, throwing. Once you get to the point that you're doing it every day, it gets easier. I've got to give a lot of thanks to Roger."

He wasn't the only Padres catcher on the elite framing list. Yasmani Grandal was worth fifteen cents to his pitchers. The Padres understood the value of stealing strikes; in spring training, they had daily video sessions with their catches to discuss pitch framing and other catching mechanics.

The study of catcher framing is still in its infancy, and it is a good idea to be skeptical of the numbers listed below. One also has to remember that much of the value of a catcher's framing skills is already reflected in a pitcher's ERA. Andrew Cashner's ERA is lower thanks to his catchers.

However, catchers don't play every day. When one sits out, it is a good idea to know how different his replacement is behind the plate.

## 2014 Pitch Framing Value

| Catcher | # Pitch/Gm | RPG | 2014 Price |
|---|---|---|---|
| Jarrod Saltalamacchia | -2.92 | -.388 | -$0.09 |
| Anthony Recker | -2.54 | -.337 | -$0.07 |
| John Jaso | -2.26 | -.300 | -$0.07 |
| Bryan Holaday | -2.04 | -.272 | -$0.06 |
| Kurt Suzuki | -1.66 | -.221 | -$0.05 |
| Dioner Navarro | -1.6 | -.213 | -$0.05 |
| Welington Castillo | -1.45 | -.193 | -$0.04 |
| Michael McKenry | -1.37 | -.183 | -$0.04 |
| A.J. Ellis | -1.36 | -.181 | -$0.04 |
| Carlos Ruiz | -0.98 | -.130 | -$0.03 |
| Salvador Perez | -0.85 | -.113 | -$0.03 |
| Robinson Chirinos | -0.77 | -.102 | -$0.02 |
| Chris Iannetta | -0.47 | -.062 | -$0.01 |
| Derek Norris | -0.4 | -.053 | -$0.01 |
| John Baker | -0.38 | -.050 | -$0.01 |
| A.J. Pierzynski | -0.32 | -.043 | -$0.01 |
| Wilin Rosario | -0.24 | -.032 | -$0.01 |
| Wilson Ramos | -0.03 | -.004 | $0.00 |
| Devin Mesoraco | 0.07 | .009 | $0.00 |
| Alex Avila | 0.24 | .031 | $0.01 |
| Jeff Mathis | 0.39 | .052 | $0.01 |
| Nick Hundley | 0.44 | .059 | $0.01 |
| Evan Gattis | 0.79 | .105 | $0.02 |
| Yadier Molina | 0.8 | .107 | $0.02 |
| Jose Lobaton | 1.31 | .175 | $0.04 |
| Ryan Hanigan | 1.47 | .196 | $0.05 |
| Tyler Flowers | 1.49 | .198 | $0.05 |
| Yan Gomes | 1.53 | .204 | $0.05 |
| Drew Butera | 1.7 | .227 | $0.05 |
| Brian McCann | 1.73 | .230 | $0.05 |
| Travis d'Arnaud | 1.75 | .233 | $0.05 |
| Jason Castro | 1.79 | .238 | $0.06 |

| Catcher | # Pitch/Gm | RPG | 2014 Price |
| --- | --- | --- | --- |
| Miguel Montero | 1.84 | .245 | $0.06 |
| Jonathan Lucroy | 2.28 | .304 | $0.07 |
| David Ross | 2.29 | .304 | $0.07 |
| Carlos Corporan | 2.52 | .335 | $0.08 |
| Russell Martin | 2.68 | .356 | $0.09 |
| Caleb Joseph | 2.9 | .386 | $0.09 |
| Mike Zunino | 3.12 | .415 | $0.10 |
| Jose Molina | 3.84 | .510 | $0.13 |
| Yasmani Grandal | 4.39 | .584 | $0.15 |
| Buster Posey | 4.62 | .614 | $0.16 |
| Christian Vazquez | 4.66 | .620 | $0.16 |
| Rene Rivera | 5.42 | .720 | $0.19 |

# THE UMPIRE ROTATION

Umpires typically move clockwise from game to game. The third base ump moves to second base, second base moves to first, the first base umpire goes to home, and the home umpire moves over to third after he calls balls and strikes. The introduction of umpire vacations, however, has caused some changes in this movement. AAA umpires usually don't umpire games behind home plate. MLB also takes advantage of doubleheaders to give umpires additional rest; an AAA umpire is often called up to work these games. In Game One, the AAA umpire usually starts at third base, then moves over to first base for the nightcap. The Game Two home plate umpire usually doesn't work the first game. The home plate umpire in the first game of the double header also gets a game off. When dealing with doubleheaders, a bettor needs to be on his toes.

# ADJUSTING YOUR TOTALS

Bob McCune, in his book "Insights into Sports Betting", advises adjusting your projected total downward by ½ run when a pitcher's umpire is behind the plate. He defines such as a home plate umpire that goes under in 60% or more of his games. When an umpire goes under 70% or more, McCune would take a full run off his expected total for the game. The opposite is true as well. I have found these adjustments an effective way to account for the home plate umpire in most instances. Many bettors will blindly bet the under when a pitcher's umpire is calling balls and strikes. This is a very big mistake. The sportsbooks know who is going to umpire home plate; they will adjust the total if they feel it is necessary. A gambler must make his own total line, tweak it according to the umpire, and only then make a play based on those numbers.

# HOMER UMPIRES

Just as there are Over umpires, there are also homer umpires. Homer umpires tend to take the path of least resistance; consciously or subconsciously, the umpire will go with the crowd and tends to call the borderline pitches for the home team. There are also umpires that will go the other way. Some enjoy being the most hated man in the ballpark, and will tend to call the close ones against the home team. Keeping accurate records again will alert you to these umpires.

Umpires all have their little quirks when they umpire games. Some umpires favor veterans; Bruce Froemming was one of these. Young players couldn't stand him for this. Others, when faced with a meaningless game in the middle of August, will go through the motions and try to get the ballgame over as quickly as possible. Some umpires will try to avoid calling a third strike; others, when a borderline pitch is thrown, will let the count affect what the call will do. If the count is 2-1, the close pitch is a strike. If the count is 1-2, the close pitch will be a ball.

Some umpires will widen the strike zone when it is hot out. A few will do so when it is cold. Some umpires will call the high curve ball for a strike. Steve Palermo, one of the best umpires in the game before he was shot and paralyzed breaking up a robbery, would reward a pitcher who showed guts in throwing a high curve ball. The opposite is true as well. Many umpires will quit on the high curve ball and not give that pitch to a pitcher.

*Success is walking from failure to failure with no loss of enthusiasm.*
*Winston Churchill*

*Positive thinking will let you do everything better than negative thinking will.*
*Zig Ziglar*

# OVER/UNDER UMPIRES

The following umpires have shown a tendency to call high scoring games or low scoring games. The hard data only tells part of the story. It is important to watch an umpire call balls and strikes for a few games before making a judgment on that umpire's strike zone.

In general, umpires who call the strike zone by the book are the ones whose games tend to go Over. Inconsistent umpires will go Under; umps who "miss" calls will usually screw up by calling a strike when the pitch should have been a ball.

| Under Umpires | Over Umpires |
|---|---|
| Jordan Baker | Lance Barrett |
| Phil Cuzzi | Angel Campos |
| Doug Eddings | Chris Conroy |
| Marty Foster | Adrian Johnson |
| John Hirschbeck | Tim McClelland |
| James Hoye | Paul Schrieber |
| Ron Kulpa | John Tumpane |
| Bill Miller | Larry Vanover |
| Mike Muchlinski | |
| DJ Reyburn | |

# WEATHER UMPIRES

It isn't easy being a home plate umpire, especially when the weather is bad. Players get a break every half inning. They are also usually much younger and in better shape. Therefore, it isn't surprising to see some umpires strike zone change when the weather isn't very good. Fluke, randomness, just plain luck, I'm not sure, but these umpires tend to have low scoring games when the weather gets nasty.

| Cold Under Umps | Hot Under Umps |
| --- | --- |
| Mark Carlson | Jordan Baker |
| Fieldin Culbreth | Phil Cuzzi |
| Rob Drake | Kerwin Danley |
| James Hoye | Bob Davidson |
| Jeff Kellogg | Mike Estabrook |
| Brian Knight | Marty Foster |
| Jerry Layne | Angel Hernandez |
| Bill Miller | James Hoye |
| Jeff Nelson | Bill Miller |
| Mike Winters | Ed Rapuano |

| Best Balls and Strikes Callers | |
| --- | --- |
| Alan Porter | Eric Cooper |
| Angel Campos | Greg Gibson |
| Brian Knight | Hal Gibson III |
| Chad Fairchild | Lance Barksdale |
| Chris Conroy | Manny Gonzalez |
| D.J. Reyburn | Paul Schrieber |
| Dana DeMuth | Tim McClelland |

| Worst Balls and Strikes Callers | |
| --- | --- |
| Bob Davidson | Kerwin Danley |
| Hunter Wendelstedt | Brian Gorman |
| Ted Barrett | Brian O'Nora |
| Paul Nauert | Lance Barrett |
| Marty Foster | Laz Diaz |
| Dan Iassogna | Angel Hernandez |
| Bill Miller | Tim Welke |

# Umpire Roster and Totals History
## (In alphabetical order)

| Umpire | Games | Over | Under | Push | Over % |
|---|---|---|---|---|---|
| Jordan Baker | 79 | 27 | 47 | 5 | 36% |
| Sean Barber | 24 | 13 | 10 | 1 | 57% |
| Lance Barksdale | 345 | 149 | 179 | 17 | 45% |
| Lance Barrett | 78 | 42 | 32 | 4 | 57% |
| Ted Barrett | 379 | 171 | 192 | 16 | 47% |
| Scott Barry | 239 | 118 | 113 | 8 | 51% |
| Toby Basner | 33 | 23 | 10 | 0 | 70% |
| Dan Bellino | 159 | 68 | 86 | 5 | 44% |
| Cory Blaser | 115 | 51 | 57 | 7 | 47% |
| Seth Buckminster | 16 | 5 | 10 | 1 | 33% |
| CB Bucknor | 370 | 181 | 170 | 19 | 52% |
| Angel Campos | 132 | 73 | 52 | 7 | 58% |
| Vic Carapazza | 141 | 59 | 74 | 8 | 44% |
| Mark Carlson | 340 | 152 | 175 | 13 | 46% |
| Gary Cederstrom | 366 | 177 | 175 | 14 | 50% |
| Chris Conroy | 108 | 56 | 48 | 4 | 54% |
| Eric Cooper | 371 | 175 | 180 | 16 | 49% |
| Fieldin Culbreth | 377 | 174 | 190 | 13 | 48% |
| Phil Cuzzi | 375 | 154 | 195 | 26 | 44% |
| Kerwin Danley | 314 | 136 | 166 | 12 | 45% |
| Bob Davidson | 349 | 159 | 173 | 17 | 48% |
| Gerry Davis | 368 | 178 | 169 | 21 | 51% |
| Dana DeMuth | 348 | 171 | 160 | 17 | 52% |
| Laz Diaz | 377 | 181 | 181 | 15 | 50% |
| Mike DiMuro | 284 | 139 | 130 | 15 | 52% |
| Rob Drake | 369 | 173 | 177 | 19 | 49% |
| Doug Eddings | 368 | 149 | 204 | 15 | 42% |
| Paul Emmel | 359 | 176 | 161 | 22 | 52% |
| Mike Estabrook | 188 | 80 | 98 | 10 | 45% |
| Mike Everitt | 371 | 173 | 185 | 13 | 48% |
| Clint Fagan | 52 | 20 | 32 | 0 | 38% |

| Umpire | Games | Over | Under | Push | Over % |
|---|---|---|---|---|---|
| Chad Fairchild | 267 | 126 | 133 | 8 | 49% |
| Andy Fletcher | 338 | 150 | 168 | 20 | 47% |
| Marty Foster | 349 | 148 | 190 | 11 | 44% |
| Greg Gibson | 366 | 168 | 181 | 17 | 48% |
| Hal Gibson III | 41 | 16 | 24 | 1 | 40% |
| Manny Gonzalez | 94 | 43 | 43 | 8 | 50% |
| Brian Gorman | 355 | 152 | 179 | 24 | 46% |
| Chris Guccione | 369 | 181 | 172 | 16 | 51% |
| Tom Hallion | 337 | 152 | 170 | 15 | 47% |
| Adam Hamari | 41 | 21 | 18 | 2 | 54% |
| Angel Hernandez | 372 | 167 | 186 | 19 | 47% |
| Ed Hickox | 278 | 130 | 137 | 11 | 49% |
| Pat Hoberg | 32 | 16 | 12 | 4 | 57% |
| James Hoye | 328 | 138 | 177 | 13 | 44% |
| Marvin Hudson | 373 | 186 | 172 | 15 | 52% |
| Dan Iassogna | 371 | 163 | 193 | 15 | 46% |
| Adrian Johnson | 248 | 125 | 108 | 15 | 54% |
| Jim Joyce | 320 | 148 | 155 | 17 | 49% |
| Jeff Kellogg | 357 | 157 | 187 | 13 | 46% |
| Brian Knight | 280 | 131 | 140 | 9 | 48% |
| Ron Kulpa | 367 | 150 | 203 | 14 | 42% |
| Jerry Layne | 324 | 145 | 164 | 15 | 47% |
| Alfonso Marquez | 333 | 151 | 165 | 17 | 48% |
| Tim McClelland | 341 | 175 | 150 | 16 | 54% |
| Jerry Meals | 376 | 184 | 167 | 25 | 52% |
| Bill Miller | 383 | 151 | 212 | 20 | 42% |
| Gabe Morales | 31 | 20 | 8 | 3 | 71% |
| Mike Muchlinski | 160 | 66 | 88 | 6 | 43% |
| Paul Nauert | 360 | 169 | 178 | 13 | 49% |
| Jeff Nelson | 361 | 158 | 185 | 18 | 46% |
| Brian O'Nora | 338 | 154 | 170 | 14 | 48% |
| Marcus Pattillo | 14 | 6 | 8 | 0 | 43% |
| Alan Porter | 133 | 59 | 71 | 3 | 45% |
| David Rackley | 62 | 27 | 29 | 6 | 48% |

| Umpire | Games | Over | Under | Push | Over % |
|---|---|---|---|---|---|
| Tony Randazzo | 322 | 153 | 150 | 19 | 50% |
| D.J. Reyburn | 135 | 56 | 72 | 7 | 44% |
| Jim Reynolds | 363 | 180 | 164 | 19 | 52% |
| Mark Ripperger | 48 | 20 | 23 | 5 | 47% |
| Paul Schrieber | 324 | 168 | 144 | 12 | 54% |
| Dale Scott | 373 | 171 | 188 | 14 | 48% |
| Chris Segal | 25 | 18 | 7 | 0 | 72% |
| Todd Tichenor | 215 | 101 | 99 | 15 | 51% |
| Tim Timmons | 364 | 165 | 175 | 24 | 49% |
| John Tumpane | 67 | 34 | 26 | 7 | 57% |
| Larry Vanover | 367 | 187 | 163 | 17 | 53% |
| Mark Wegner | 349 | 165 | 165 | 19 | 50% |
| Bill Welke | 363 | 167 | 180 | 16 | 48% |
| Tim Welke | 359 | 167 | 174 | 18 | 49% |
| Hunter Wendelstedt | 345 | 170 | 161 | 14 | 51% |
| Joe West | 386 | 190 | 175 | 21 | 52% |
| Mike Winters | 361 | 160 | 187 | 14 | 46% |
| Quinn Wolcott | 47 | 25 | 21 | 1 | 54% |
| Jim Wolf | 348 | 157 | 169 | 22 | 48% |
| Tom Woodring | 23 | 12 | 10 | 1 | 55% |

# UMPIRE OVER/UNDER HISTORY
(From lowest Over % to highest)

| Umpire | Games | Over | Under | Push | Over % |
|---|---|---|---|---|---|
| Seth Buckminster | 16 | 5 | 10 | 1 | 33% |
| Jordan Baker | 79 | 27 | 47 | 5 | 36% |
| Clint Fagan | 52 | 20 | 32 | 0 | 38% |
| Hal Gibson III | 41 | 16 | 24 | 1 | 40% |
| Bill Miller | 383 | 151 | 212 | 20 | 42% |
| Doug Eddings | 368 | 149 | 204 | 15 | 42% |
| Ron Kulpa | 367 | 150 | 203 | 14 | 42% |
| Mike Muchlinski | 160 | 66 | 88 | 6 | 43% |
| Marcus Pattillo | 14 | 6 | 8 | 0 | 43% |
| D.J. Reyburn | 135 | 56 | 72 | 7 | 44% |
| Marty Foster | 349 | 148 | 190 | 11 | 44% |
| James Hoye | 328 | 138 | 177 | 13 | 44% |
| Phil Cuzzi | 375 | 154 | 195 | 26 | 44% |
| Dan Bellino | 159 | 68 | 86 | 5 | 44% |
| Vic Carapazza | 141 | 59 | 74 | 8 | 44% |
| Mike Estabrook | 188 | 80 | 98 | 10 | 45% |
| Kerwin Danley | 314 | 136 | 166 | 12 | 45% |
| Alan Porter | 133 | 59 | 71 | 3 | 45% |
| Lance Barksdale | 345 | 149 | 179 | 17 | 45% |
| Jeff Kellogg | 357 | 157 | 187 | 13 | 46% |
| Dan Iassogna | 371 | 163 | 193 | 15 | 46% |
| Brian Gorman | 355 | 152 | 179 | 24 | 46% |
| Jeff Nelson | 361 | 158 | 185 | 18 | 46% |
| Mike Winters | 361 | 160 | 187 | 14 | 46% |
| Mark Carlson | 340 | 152 | 175 | 13 | 46% |
| Mark Ripperger | 48 | 20 | 23 | 5 | 47% |
| Jerry Layne | 324 | 145 | 164 | 15 | 47% |
| Ted Barrett | 379 | 171 | 192 | 16 | 47% |
| Andy Fletcher | 338 | 150 | 168 | 20 | 47% |
| Tom Hallion | 337 | 152 | 170 | 15 | 47% |
| Cory Blaser | 115 | 51 | 57 | 7 | 47% |

| Umpire | Games | Over | Under | Push | Over % |
|---|---|---|---|---|---|
| Angel Hernandez | 372 | 167 | 186 | 19 | 47% |
| Brian O'Nora | 338 | 154 | 170 | 14 | 48% |
| Dale Scott | 373 | 171 | 188 | 14 | 48% |
| Alfonso Marquez | 333 | 151 | 165 | 17 | 48% |
| Fieldin Culbreth | 377 | 174 | 190 | 13 | 48% |
| Bob Davidson | 349 | 159 | 173 | 17 | 48% |
| Bill Welke | 363 | 167 | 180 | 16 | 48% |
| Greg Gibson | 366 | 168 | 181 | 17 | 48% |
| Jim Wolf | 348 | 157 | 169 | 22 | 48% |
| David Rackley | 62 | 27 | 29 | 6 | 48% |
| Mike Everitt | 371 | 173 | 185 | 13 | 48% |
| Brian Knight | 280 | 131 | 140 | 9 | 48% |
| Tim Timmons | 364 | 165 | 175 | 24 | 49% |
| Chad Fairchild | 267 | 126 | 133 | 8 | 49% |
| Ed Hickox | 278 | 130 | 137 | 11 | 49% |
| Paul Nauert | 360 | 169 | 178 | 13 | 49% |
| Jim Joyce | 320 | 148 | 155 | 17 | 49% |
| Tim Welke | 359 | 167 | 174 | 18 | 49% |
| Eric Cooper | 371 | 175 | 180 | 16 | 49% |
| Rob Drake | 369 | 173 | 177 | 19 | 49% |
| Laz Diaz | 377 | 181 | 181 | 15 | 50% |
| Manny Gonzalez | 94 | 43 | 43 | 8 | 50% |
| Mark Wegner | 349 | 165 | 165 | 19 | 50% |
| Gary Cederstrom | 366 | 177 | 175 | 14 | 50% |
| Tony Randazzo | 322 | 153 | 150 | 19 | 50% |
| Todd Tichenor | 215 | 101 | 99 | 15 | 51% |
| Scott Barry | 239 | 118 | 113 | 8 | 51% |
| Chris Guccione | 369 | 181 | 172 | 16 | 51% |
| Gerry Davis | 368 | 178 | 169 | 21 | 51% |
| Hunter Wendelstedt | 345 | 170 | 161 | 14 | 51% |
| CB Bucknor | 370 | 181 | 170 | 19 | 52% |
| Dana DeMuth | 348 | 171 | 160 | 17 | 52% |

| Umpire | Games | Over | Under | Push | Over % |
|---|---|---|---|---|---|
| Mike DiMuro | 284 | 139 | 130 | 15 | 52% |
| Marvin Hudson | 373 | 186 | 172 | 15 | 52% |
| | | | | | |
| **Umpire** | **Games** | **Over** | **Under** | **Push** | **Over %** |
| Joe West | 386 | 190 | 175 | 21 | 52% |
| Paul Emmel | 359 | 176 | 161 | 22 | 52% |
| Jim Reynolds | 363 | 180 | 164 | 19 | 52% |
| Jerry Meals | 376 | 184 | 167 | 25 | 52% |
| Larry Vanover | 367 | 187 | 163 | 17 | 53% |
| Adrian Johnson | 248 | 125 | 108 | 15 | 54% |
| Chris Conroy | 108 | 56 | 48 | 4 | 54% |
| Adam Hamari | 41 | 21 | 18 | 2 | 54% |
| Tim McClelland | 341 | 175 | 150 | 16 | 54% |
| Paul Schrieber | 324 | 168 | 144 | 12 | 54% |
| Quinn Wolcott | 47 | 25 | 21 | 1 | 54% |
| Tom Woodring | 23 | 12 | 10 | 1 | 55% |
| Sean Barber | 24 | 13 | 10 | 1 | 57% |
| John Tumpane | 67 | 34 | 26 | 7 | 57% |
| Lance Barrett | 78 | 42 | 32 | 4 | 57% |
| Pat Hoberg | 32 | 16 | 12 | 4 | 57% |
| Angel Campos | 132 | 73 | 52 | 7 | 58% |
| Toby Basner | 33 | 23 | 10 | 0 | 70% |
| Gabe Morales | 31 | 20 | 8 | 3 | 71% |
| Chris Segal | 25 | 18 | 7 | 0 | 72% |

# PARK EFFECTS

A home run hit in Coors Field is not equal to a homer hit in Dodger Stadium. This concept, known as the park effect, states that statistics like runs, ERA, batting average and so on, are all dependent in part on the environment of a specific park. Coors Field has been the most hitter friendly park in baseball the last few years, followed by the Ballpark in Arlington, Chase Field in Arizona, and U.S. Cellular Field for the White Sox. Pitchers from these teams are generally better than a number like ERA indicates, and the offense in comparison isn't quite as powerful as one might suspect.

A handicapper has several methods he can use to establish a team's true park factor. Base Park Index is the simplest; it involves eight steps:

| | CALCULATING PARK FACTORS |
|---|---|
| Step 1 | Add The Total Runs Scored In Home Park |
| Step 2 | Add The Total At-Bats In Home Park |
| Step 3 | Divide Step 1 By Step 2 |
| Step 4 | Add The Total Runs Scored In Away Games |
| Step 5 | Add The Total At-Bats In Away Games |
| Step 6 | Divide Step 4 By Step 5 |
| Step 7 | Divide Step 5 By Step 6 |

This typically gives a number ranging from 90% to 110%. If a ballpark's number is 100%, then it is a league average park. A 110% number means that it is a hitter's park; 10% more runs are scored at that stadium than a league average park. A 90% number means the park has decreased scoring by 10%.

It is advisable to calculate park factors for more than one year; random fluctuations will often play havoc with your park factors if you use only one year. Five-year data pools tend to be the most accurate. Many handicappers, however, believe three years' worth of data is enough to smooth out the chance factor. Weather fluctuates from year to year. An unusually hot and dry summer will increase scoring. Wind patterns shift from year to year as well. These are just a few examples as to what may adversely affect the accuracy of Park Factors.

It is also a reason why precision regarding park factors isn't necessary or even wanted. A bettor should go into each day's game with an open mind as to how that park will play that game. If the wind is kicking up, or a cold streak coming through town, that five-year data pool doesn't mean much.

Park factors help filter out the bias that a team has from playing in an extreme pitcher/hitter park. It is only a tool, however, and not complete accurate one at that. AT&T Park may depress home runs from left-handed hitters overall, but Barry Bonds certainly wasn't affected too much by his home park.

A good example of the strangeness of park factors is the Sportsman's Park experience. Bill Febler, in "The Book on the Book", details this story. Before moving to Baltimore, the St. Louis Browns shared Sportsman's Park with the St. Louis Cardinals. Since both teams shared the same stadium, one would assume that the park factor would be generally the same. Not true. In the 33 years that the two teams shared the stadium, the Browns had a park factor of 114%. The Cardinals' park factor was only 107%.

The numbers varied widely when looking at specific years. In 1920, the Cardinals had a 99% park factor. The Browns saw an increase of scoring by 24%, one of the best offensive parks in the American League. The 33-year history saw other similar occurrences. In 1938, the Cardinals had a park factor of 138%. The Browns' park factor was only 104%.

This wasn't just limited to St. Louis. When the Yankees and Mets shared Shea Stadium for two years in the 1970's, the home park factors for each team varied widely. The Phillies and A's saw similar results when those two clubs shared the same park. Park factors aren't perfect, and be cautious before relying on them. Nevertheless, don't discount it. This 'best guess' tool is a valuable piece of handicapping.

If Petco Field in San Diego deflates run scoring by 16%, then the park factor is 84%. To adjust a Padres pitcher's stats for park factor, you will have to divide its run inflation (or deflation) rate (-16%) by two to account for the fact that the player plays half his games at home.

For example, Ian Kennedy had a 3.23 ERA in 2014 pitching for San Diego. Accounting for San Diego's 84% park factor would show Correia's adjusted ERA to be 3.49. It is still a respectable number, but not as impressive as his raw ERA.

| Step 1: | 100%-84% | 16% |
|---------|----------|-----|
| Step 2: | Divide Step 1 by 2 | 8% |
| Step 3: | Step 2 * 3.23 | .26 |
| Step 4: | Step 3 + 3.23 | 3.49 ERA |

Let's try this with Jhoulys Chacin, a Colorado Rockies pitcher with a 5.40 ERA in 2014. Colorado inflates offense about 40% over the past five years.

| Step 1: | 100%-140% | -40% |
|---------|-----------|------|
| Step 2: | Divide Step 1 by 2 | -20% |
| Step 3: | Step 2 * 5.40 | -1.08 |
| Step 4: | Step 3 + 5.40 | 4.32 ERA |

These adjustments aren't perfect, and a bettor shouldn't always trust the numbers. The unbalanced schedule throws a wrench into these calculations as well. It is, however, a reasonable way to judge how the perception of a pitcher may be wrong because of that pitcher's home ballpark. Chacin was bad in 2014, but not as awful as his raw numbers suggest.

Park factors aren't infallible, and can vary from week to week, day to day, even from inning to inning. It isn't rare to see the wind that was gusting out to left field at Wrigley flip in the beginning of the game flip around and blow in later in the game. It is an average, and average can be dangerous things

# HOME FIELD ADVANTAGE
# BALLPARK LAYOUTS

Home teams win about 58% of the time in the NFL. In the NHL, home teams win about 63%. Pro basketball sees its home fans go home happy around 60% of the time. Baseball doesn't have that huge advantage. On average, home teams win 54% of the time.

The reasons for baseball's home field advantage are unclear: friendly fans, familiarity with a stadium's unique characteristics and umpiring bias towards the home team have all been mentioned as possible reasons a home team is better at home.

Whatever the reason, a bettor needs to account for this advantage. The typical bonus price for home field advantage is 16 to 18 cents. In other words, if two evenly matched teams were playing, the home team would be about a -117 favorite.

It is just a generic rule of thumb, however. Some teams deserve more, and some deserve less. That's where one should focus. By concentrating on the outliers, a handicapper can grind out a few more bets and avoid plays that the numbers would otherwise indicate as offering good value.

It is also vital to know which way the wind is when betting on a specific pitcher or a total. Fly ball pitchers will be helped if the wind is  blowing in, and are penalized if the wind is gusting out. The ballpark layouts on the following pages show the direction of each stadium. The bottom shows south; the right side is east, the left side is west, and the top is north. As an example, the layout to the left has home plate to first base running north to south. Wind blowing out of the north means it is blowing out to right field.

# CHASE FIELD, ARIZONA

Due to the Arizona heat, Chase Field's roof typically is closed during the summer while the air conditioning is kept going full speed. With the roof shut and the air conditioning running, the ball doesn't carry as well. When the roof is open, run scoring will usually be inflated. Even when closed, however, the stadium is a hitter's ballpark. Chase Field has an elevation 1,100 above sea level, the second highest stadium in the majors behind Coors Field in Denver. The high altitude and a great hitter's background are big factors in the high number of runs scored in Chase. While the foul territory is large and gives an occasional boost to the pitcher, the other factors more than make up for the loss. Run scoring took a dive in 2013 at Chase but bounced up to normal range in 2014. Still, there is no sustained edge in betting Overs at Chase.

| PARK NAME | Year | RUNS | HR | H | 2B | 3B | BB |
|---|---|---|---|---|---|---|---|
| Chase Field | 2010 | 105% | 106% | 105% | 105% | 230% | 94% |
| Chase Field | 2011 | 115% | 110% | 106% | 115% | 138% | 93% |
| Chase Field | 2012 | 117% | 119% | 106% | 118% | 118% | 96% |
| Chase Field | 2013 | 97% | 95% | 94% | 101% | 138% | 98% |
| Chase Field | 2014 | 115% | 119% | 105% | 108% | 179% | 94% |
| 5 Year Average | | 110% | 110% | 103% | 109% | 160% | 95% |

| Year | Over | Under | Push | Over % | Under % | RF | RA |
|---|---|---|---|---|---|---|---|
| 2010 | 42 | 37 | 2 | 53% | 47% | 4.7 | 5 |
| 2011 | 36 | 44 | 3 | 45% | 55% | 5 | 4.2 |
| 2012 | 39 | 38 | 4 | 51% | 49% | 4.8 | 4.6 |
| 2013 | 34 | 45 | 2 | 43% | 57% | 4.2 | 4.2 |
| 2014 | 37 | 38 | 4 | 49% | 51% | 4.3 | 4.7 |
| Total | 188 | 202 | 15 | 48% | 52% | 4.6 | 4.5 |

# Arizona

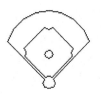

The Diamondbacks lost a whopping 23.4 units on the road last year thanks to their 25-56 record. This isn't a surprise. Since joining the National League in 1997, Arizona has had a winning road record in just four of the 13 seasons. The depth of the ineptitude last year was impressive, however. Only the 2004 team had a worse winning percentage on the road.

| Year | Hm Win | Hm Loss | Win % | Units | Rd Win | Rd Loss | Win % | Units |
|------|--------|---------|-------|-------|--------|---------|-------|-------|
| 2010 | 40 | 41 | 49% | -2.1 | 25 | 56 | 31% | -23 |
| 2011 | 53 | 30 | 64% | 16 | 43 | 41 | 51% | 10 |
| 2012 | 41 | 40 | 51% | -14 | 40 | 41 | 49% | 1.8 |
| 2013 | 45 | 36 | 56% | -1.2 | 36 | 45 | 44% | -3.6 |
| 2014 | 33 | 46 | 42% | -17 | 31 | 52 | 37% | -15 |
| Total | 212 | 193 | 52% | -18 | 175 | 235 | 43% | -30 |

# TURNER FIELD, ATLANTA

Turner Field was originally built as the main stadium for the 1996 Olympic Games in Atlanta. Once the Games were over, the Braves converted the stadium into a modern day ballpark with suites and luxury boxes. The stadium is doomed, however. The Braves are building a new stadium in Cobb County and will begin play there in 2017. Turner Field is a pitcher friendly park that hurts left-handed power hitters and teams without speed in center and right field. Spring winds and cool air can keep scoring down early, but the high altitude and wind blowing through the open centerfield area help the ball carry on warmer days. The park has leaned Under in recent years.

| PARK NAME | Year | RUNS | HR | H | 2B | 3B | BB |
|---|---|---|---|---|---|---|---|
| Turner Field | 2010 | 101% | 102% | 100% | 93% | 90% | 92% |
| Turner Field | 2011 | 95% | 95% | 101% | 98% | 63% | 106% |
| Turner Field | 2012 | 104% | 87% | 101% | 120% | 104% | 104% |
| Turner Field | 2013 | 96% | 93% | 99% | 92% | 125% | 95% |
| Turner Field | 2014 | 94% | 112% | 97% | 83% | 63% | 101% |
| 5 Yr. Average | | 98% | 98% | 100% | 97% | 89% | 99% |

| Year | Over | Under | Push | Over % | Under % | RF | RA |
|---|---|---|---|---|---|---|---|
| 2010 | 36 | 42 | 5 | 46% | 54% | 4.8 | 3.6 |
| 2011 | 34 | 40 | 7 | 46% | 54% | 4 | 3.5 |
| 2012 | 35 | 45 | 2 | 44% | 56% | 4.3 | 3.9 |
| 2013 | 35 | 43 | 5 | 45% | 55% | 4.4 | 3.0 |
| 2014 | 33 | 40 | 8 | 45% | 55% | 3.5 | 3.5 |
| Total | 173 | 210 | 27 | 45% | 55% | 4.2 | 3.5 |

# Atlanta

The Braves rode a strong home field advantage to 97 wins in 2013, but that edge faded in 2014. Atlanta lost 9.4 units at home last year, and 8.3 units on the road. That is likely a fluke; the Braves had been one of the more profitable home teams in baseball in recent years.

| Year | Hm Win | Hm Loss | Win % | Units | Rd Win | Rd Loss | Win % | Units |
|------|--------|---------|-------|-------|--------|---------|-------|-------|
| 2010 | 56 | 27 | 68% | 13.3 | 36 | 47 | 43% | -17 |
| 2011 | 47 | 34 | 58% | -3.1 | 42 | 39 | 52% | -0.1 |
| 2012 | 48 | 34 | 59% | 2.3 | 46 | 35 | 57% | 13.1 |
| 2013 | 57 | 26 | 69% | 15.9 | 40 | 43 | 48% | -7.9 |
| 2014 | 42 | 39 | 52% | -9.4 | 37 | 44 | 46% | -8.3 |
| Total | 250 | 160 | 61% | 19 | 201 | 208 | 49% | -20 |

# CAMDEN YARDS, BALTIMORE

Camden Yards set the standard when it comes to new baseball stadiums. Built in 1992, Camden was once considered a pitcher's park. No more, even if scoring took a dive in 2014. Home runs are plentiful here; the ball does tend to carry when the weather heats up. Baltimore typically grows the infield grass higher than most ballparks, helping ground ball pitchers as well as teams with infielders that lacking in range. While right-handed batters love taking a shot at the 364-foot fence in left center, left-handed bats are the ones that enjoy most of the power boost from Camden Yards.

| PARK NAME | Year | RUNS | HR | H | 2B | 3B | BB |
|---|---|---|---|---|---|---|---|
| Camden Yards | 2010 | 111% | 126% | 108% | 101% | 71% | 101% |
| Camden Yards | 2011 | 100% | 114% | 99% | 109% | 74% | 104% |
| Camden Yards | 2012 | 117% | 131% | 110% | 107% | 68% | 103% |
| Camden Yards | 2013 | 106% | 128% | 99% | 86% | 64% | 101% |
| Camden Yards | 2014 | 93% | 94% | 98% | 94% | 64% | 100% |
| 5 Year Average | | 105% | 119% | 103% | 99% | 68% | 102% |

| Year | Over | Under | Push | Over % | Under % | RF | RA |
|---|---|---|---|---|---|---|---|
| 2006 | 43 | 38 | 0 | 53% | 47% | 5.1 | 5.1 |
| 2007 | 45 | 33 | 3 | 58% | 42% | 4.8 | 5.8 |
| 2008 | 38 | 36 | 6 | 51% | 49% | 5.0 | 5.5 |
| 2009 | 35 | 44 | 2 | 44% | 56% | 5.1 | 5.1 |
| 2010 | 34 | 42 | 5 | 45% | 55% | 4.0 | 5.1 |
| Total | 195 | 193 | 16 | 50% | 50% | 4.8 | 5.3 |

# Baltimore

Baltimore won both home and away last year, finishing a whopping +34 units on the season. Showalter typically has his team ready to play at all times, so I don't expect any massive home/away splits that you see from some teams. Since Showalter took over in 2010, the O's have won 54% of their home games and 47% of their road games.

| Year | Hm Win | Hm Loss | Win % | Units | Rd Win | Rd Loss | Win % | Units |
|------|--------|---------|-------|-------|--------|---------|-------|-------|
| 2010 | 37 | 44 | 46% | -0.4 | 29 | 52 | 36% | -1.6 |
| 2011 | 39 | 42 | 48% | 2 | 30 | 51 | 37% | -7.4 |
| 2012 | 48 | 35 | 58% | 10.6 | 48 | 37 | 57% | 27.8 |
| 2013 | 46 | 35 | 57% | 0.4 | 39 | 42 | 48% | -0.3 |
| 2014 | 52 | 33 | 61% | 14.1 | 47 | 37 | 56% | 20.2 |
| Total | 222 | 189 | 54% | 26.7 | 193 | 219 | 47% | 38.7 |

# FENWAY PARK, BOSTON

There are no cheap outs in Fenway. The small foul grounds and short field means a pitcher cannot make a mistake without paying for it. It also means fans rather than players in the field catch foul pop flies. The 17-foot wall in centerfield helps hitters by providing a great hitting background. Then you have the Green Monster, which turns routine fly balls into extra-base hits. It is deadly to a left-handed junk baller. Pitchers who get their own outs via the strikeout will do better in this ballpark than a control pitcher who must rely on his defense to get him out of trouble. Lefties have always had a tough time hitting home runs in Fenway. What is new is the difficulties right-handed hitters have recently had hitting the long ball.

| PARK NAME | Year | RUNS | HR | H | 2B | 3B | BB |
|---|---|---|---|---|---|---|---|
| Fenway Park | 2010 | 108% | 87% | 103% | 122% | 57% | 102% |
| Fenway Park | 2011 | 117% | 88% | 116% | 131% | 115% | 98% |
| Fenway Park | 2012 | 121% | 109% | 117% | 149% | 139% | 104% |
| Fenway Park | 2013 | 96% | 85% | 100% | 118% | 129% | 92% |
| Fenway Park | 2014 | 107% | 72% | 107% | 152% | 86% | 117% |
| 5 Year Average | | 110% | 88% | 109% | 135% | 105% | 102% |

| Year | Over | Under | Push | Over % | Under % | RF | RA |
|---|---|---|---|---|---|---|---|
| 2010 | 42 | 36 | 3 | 54% | 46% | 5.2 | 4.9 |
| 2011 | 46 | 31 | 4 | 60% | 40% | 5.7 | 5.1 |
| 2012 | 42 | 34 | 5 | 55% | 45% | 5.2 | 5.2 |
| 2013 | 38 | 45 | 6 | 46% | 54% | 5.2 | 3.8 |
| 2014 | 36 | 44 | 1 | 45% | 55% | 4.0 | 4.6 |
| Total | 204 | 190 | 19 | 52% | 48% | 5.1 | 4.7 |

# Boston

Boston used to have one of the better home field advantages in baseball, taking advantage of the unique characteristics of Fenway Park. That hasn't been the case in recent years, especially with last season's disastrous home record. Since 2010, the Red Sox have lost 54 units at home; 25 of those units were lost in 2014.

| Year | Hm Win | Hm Loss | Win % | Units | Rd Win | Rd Loss | Win % | Units |
|------|--------|---------|-------|-------|--------|---------|-------|-------|
| 2010 | 46 | 35 | 57% | -4.2 | 43 | 38 | 53% | 1 |
| 2011 | 45 | 36 | 56% | -15 | 45 | 36 | 56% | 0.9 |
| 2012 | 34 | 47 | 42% | -27 | 35 | 46 | 43% | -11 |
| 2013 | 59 | 30 | 66% | 15.9 | 49 | 40 | 55% | 8.5 |
| 2014 | 34 | 47 | 42% | -25 | 37 | 44 | 46% | -2.2 |
| Total | 218 | 195 | 53% | -54 | 209 | 204 | 51% | -3 |

# U.S. CELLULAR, CHICAGO WHITE SOX

The Cell has undertaken major renovations since the 2001 season, attempting to fix some of the horrible mistakes that occurred when the stadium was built in the early 90's. The upper deck was reworked in 2004, playing havoc with wind conditions at times. It became a power park after the White Sox moved the fences in before the 2001 season. The infield is usually in good shape. Fly-ball pitchers dread this place, especially left-handers.

| PARK NAME | Year | RUNS | HR | H | 2B | 3B | BB |
|---|---|---|---|---|---|---|---|
| Cellular Field | 2010 | 114% | 155% | 100% | 112% | 78% | 117% |
| Cellular Field | 2011 | 99% | 123% | 96% | 88% | 68% | 124% |
| Cellular Field | 2012 | 127% | 135% | 108% | 113% | 89% | 121% |
| Cellular Field | 2013 | 100% | 119% | 95% | 76% | 41% | 116% |
| Cellular Field | 2014 | 105% | 105% | 101% | 100% | 110% | 105% |
| 5 Year Average | | 108% | 120% | 100% | 94% | 77% | 116% |

| Year | Over | Under | Push | Over % | Under % | RF | RA |
|---|---|---|---|---|---|---|---|
| 2010 | 44 | 33 | 4 | 57% | 43% | 5.0 | 4.6 |
| 2011 | 34 | 39 | 8 | 47% | 53% | 3.9 | 4.5 |
| 2012 | 44 | 34 | 3 | 56% | 44% | 5.1 | 4.7 |
| 2013 | 31 | 42 | 8 | 43% | 58% | 3.7 | 4.4 |
| 2014 | 43 | 37 | 1 | 54% | 46% | 4.1 | 4.8 |
| Total | 196 | 185 | 24 | 51% | 49% | 4.4 | 4.6 |

# Chicago White Sox

Chicago broke even on the money line in its home games in 2014, despite having a losing record. They also didn't lose much money on the road even going 33-48. That tells you how the bettors felt about Chicago. Historically, the White Sox do not have a very large home field advantage.

| Year | Hm Win | Hm Loss | Win % | Units | Rd Win | Rd Loss | Win % | Units |
|-------|--------|---------|-------|-------|--------|---------|-------|-------|
| 2010 | 45 | 36 | 56% | -0.1 | 43 | 38 | 53% | 10.8 |
| 2011 | 36 | 45 | 44% | -21 | 43 | 38 | 53% | 9.5 |
| 2012 | 45 | 36 | 56% | -0.3 | 40 | 41 | 49% | 1.8 |
| 2013 | 37 | 44 | 46% | -9.8 | 26 | 55 | 32% | -22 |
| 2014 | 40 | 41 | 49% | 0.5 | 33 | 48 | 41% | -1.2 |
| Total | 203 | 202 | 50% | -30 | 185 | 220 | 46% | -1.4 |

# WRIGLEY FIELD, CHICAGO CUBS

Just look to the weather to decide how Wrigley Field is going to play. When the wind blows off the lake, scoring is down. When it blows out, the scoring soars. The problem with Wrigley Field weather is everyone knows about it. When the wind is gusting in, the line typically is set too low to take advantage of the wind. Often times, the value is taking the Over when the wind is blowing in, and the Under when the wind is blowing out. The Cubs have done some work on the park in recent years, adding seats on the 3rd base line, lowering the field 14 inches (making fences higher in the process) and adding seats in the outfield bleachers. A massive $575 million renovation project started up after the end of the 2014 season. The project should take four years but shouldn't affect how the stadium plays on the field. That's to be determined, however. The Cubs have already announced project delays in the left field bleachers.

| PARK NAME | Year | RUNS | HR | H | 2B | 3B | BB |
|---|---|---|---|---|---|---|---|
| Wrigley Field | 2010 | 117% | 113% | 112% | 108% | 127% | 102% |
| Wrigley Field | 2011 | 93% | 99% | 98% | 86% | 132% | 105% |
| Wrigley Field | 2012 | 102% | 96% | 98% | 108% | 93% | 113% |
| Wrigley Field | 2013 | 119% | 112% | 110% | 112% | 89% | 104% |
| Wrigley Field | 2014 | 93% | 94% | 98% | 107% | 104% | 100% |
| 5 Year Average | | 105% | 103% | 103% | 104% | 109% | 105% |

| Year | Over | Under | Push | Over % | Under % | RF | RA |
|---|---|---|---|---|---|---|---|
| 2010 | 36 | 41 | 4 | 47% | 53% | 4.3 | 5.3 |
| 2011 | 33 | 44 | 4 | 43% | 57% | 4.0 | 4.4 |
| 2012 | 35 | 43 | 3 | 45% | 55% | 4.1 | 4.5 |
| 2013 | 37 | 39 | 5 | 49% | 51% | 4.1 | 4.5 |
| 2014 | 39 | 41 | 1 | 49% | 51% | 3.8 | 4.1 |
| Total | 180 | 208 | 17 | 46% | 54% | 4.1 | 4.6 |

# Chicago Cubs

The Cubs held their own at home in 2014, finishing one game above .500 and winning 2.4 units in the process. Even their away record wasn't horrible; Chicago lost only six units despite going 32-49. The Cubs generally have a weaker home field advantage than other major league teams, but big changes have come to the team and there is some hope for the future. That may translate into a stronger HFA.

| Year | Hm Win | Hm Loss | Win % | Units | Rd Win | Rd Loss | Win % | Units |
|------|--------|---------|-------|-------|--------|---------|-------|-------|
| 2010 | 35 | 46 | 43% | -23 | 40 | 41 | 49% | 6 |
| 2011 | 39 | 42 | 48% | -5.9 | 32 | 49 | 40% | -9.5 |
| 2012 | 38 | 43 | 47% | -2 | 23 | 58 | 28% | -24 |
| 2013 | 31 | 50 | 38% | -20 | 35 | 46 | 43% | 4.9 |
| 2014 | 41 | 40 | 51% | 2.4 | 32 | 49 | 40% | -6.1 |
| Total | 184 | 221 | 45% | -49 | 162 | 243 | 40% | -29 |

# GREAT AMERICAN BALLPARK, CINCINNATI

It is difficult to get a good read on Great American Ballpark. When it first opened in 2003, it was a pitcher's park. It then became one of the better hitter's park in baseball. The last two seasons have seen run scoring drop, even with an inflated number of home runs hit in the stadium. Fly-ball pitchers walk a fine line in this stadium due to its small fences. Strikeout pitchers do well, especially since the park seems to increase strikeouts. Pay close attention to the weather; this is one of those major league stadiums where the scoring is heavily impacted by weather conditions.

| PARK NAME | Year | RUNS | HR | H | 2B | 3B | BB |
|---|---|---|---|---|---|---|---|
| Great Am. Ball Park | 2010 | 101% | 114% | 102% | 94% | 100% | 102% |
| Great Am. Ball Park | 2011 | 108% | 131% | 99% | 85% | 70% | 91% |
| Great Am. Ball Park | 2012 | 111% | 159% | 102% | 85% | 117% | 104% |
| Great Am. Ball Park | 2013 | 99% | 134% | 99% | 108% | 82% | 100% |
| Great Am. Ball Park | 2014 | 96% | 128% | 96% | 90% | 111% | 111% |
| 5 Year Average | | 103% | 133% | 100% | 92% | 96% | 101% |

| Year | Over | Under | Push | Over % | Under % | RF | RA |
|---|---|---|---|---|---|---|---|
| 2010 | 39 | 37 | 6 | 51% | 49% | 4.9 | 4.2 |
| 2011 | 44 | 30 | 7 | 60% | 41% | 4.8 | 4.5 |
| 2012 | 35 | 41 | 8 | 46% | 54% | 4.3 | 3.9 |
| 2013 | 36 | 41 | 4 | 47% | 53% | 4.2 | 3.7 |
| 2014 | 33 | 44 | 4 | 43% | 57% | 3.8 | 3.5 |
| Total | 187 | 193 | 29 | 49% | 51% | 4.4 | 4.0 |

# Cincinnati

The Reds had been one of the stronger road teams in baseball (relative to its home performance), but that wasn't the case in 2014. Cincinnati was a disaster on the road, losing 13 units and finishing 17 games below .500. They typically play well at the Great American, but that is reflected in the lines. The Reds have won just 3.2 units in the past five years despite winning 57% of their home games.

| Year | Hm Win | Hm Loss | Win % | Units | Rd Win | Rd Loss | Win % | Units |
|-------|--------|---------|-------|-------|--------|---------|-------|-------|
| 2010 | 49 | 33 | 60% | 7.5 | 42 | 41 | 51% | 4 |
| 2011 | 42 | 39 | 52% | -8.9 | 37 | 44 | 46% | -6.3 |
| 2012 | 50 | 34 | 60% | 2.7 | 49 | 34 | 59% | 13.2 |
| 2013 | 49 | 32 | 61% | -0.9 | 41 | 41 | 50% | -5.3 |
| 2014 | 44 | 37 | 54% | 2.8 | 32 | 49 | 40% | -13 |
| Total | 234 | 175 | 57% | 3.2 | 201 | 209 | 49% | -7.7 |

# PROGRESSIVE FIELD, CLEVELAND

Teams loaded with left-handed bats can have a slight advantage at Jacobs Field, especially in warmer weather when the wind blows out. The 17-foot fence in left field keeps a large number of potential home runs in the ballpark, hurting right-handed hitters. While the park doesn't affect a team's home run rate overall, it is generally a pitcher's park. Triples are rare, and walks are routinely below the major league average.

| PARK NAME | Year | RUNS | HR | H | 2B | 3B | BB |
|---|---|---|---|---|---|---|---|
| Progressive Field | 2010 | 95% | 95% | 97% | 109% | 113% | 98% |
| Progressive Field | 2011 | 96% | 106% | 99% | 98% | 63% | 97% |
| Progressive Field | 2012 | 90% | 93% | 99% | 104% | 33% | 96% |
| Progressive Field | 2013 | 93% | 108% | 98% | 100% | 63% | 92% |
| Progressive Field | 2014 | 95% | 108% | 98% | 103% | 53% | 96% |
| 5 Year Average | | 94% | 102% | 98% | 103% | 65% | 96% |

| Year | Over | Under | Push | Over % | Under % | RF | RA |
|---|---|---|---|---|---|---|---|
| 2010 | 34 | 45 | 2 | 43% | 57% | 4.0 | 4.4 |
| 2011 | 40 | 39 | 2 | 51% | 49% | 4.3 | 4.6 |
| 2012 | 38 | 40 | 3 | 49% | 51% | 4.0 | 4.9 |
| 2013 | 40 | 40 | 2 | 50% | 50% | 4.4 | 4.0 |
| 2014 | 38 | 41 | 2 | 48% | 52% | 4.0 | 4.0 |
| Total | 190 | 205 | 11 | 48% | 52% | 4.1 | 4.4 |

# Cleveland

Cleveland has used a strong HFA to contend for the playoffs over the past two years. The Indians have won 22 units at home since 2013, going 99-64 in the process. They have struggled a bit on the road, however. The Indians lost 4.7 units last year while away from Progressive Field.

| Year | Hm Win | Hm Loss | Win % | Units | Rd Win | Rd Loss | Win % | Units |
|-------|--------|---------|-------|-------|--------|---------|-------|-------|
| 2010 | 38 | 43 | 47% | -0.6 | 31 | 50 | 38% | -4.6 |
| 2011 | 44 | 37 | 54% | 3.2 | 36 | 45 | 44% | -1.4 |
| 2012 | 37 | 44 | 46% | -9.7 | 31 | 50 | 38% | -11 |
| 2013 | 51 | 31 | 62% | 15.8 | 41 | 40 | 51% | 8.4 |
| 2014 | 48 | 33 | 59% | 6.1 | 37 | 44 | 46% | -4.7 |
| Total | 218 | 188 | 54% | 14.8 | 176 | 229 | 43% | -14 |

# COORS FIELD, DENVER

A team will struggle if it doesn't have quick outfielders in Coors. Deeper fences mean more gaps, and pitchers that can't create their own outs via strikeouts typically struggle. Walks are a killer in Coors. Avoid pitchers who can't throw strikes. Right-handed batters thrive in this park. Home runs had dropped sharply in 2013 but that turned out to be a fluke; 2014 saw a big increase in home runs and run scoring. It is not easy to strike out hitters in Coors. Rule of thumb: never bet the Under at Coors.

| PARK NAME | Year | RUNS | HR | H | 2B | 3B | BB |
|---|---|---|---|---|---|---|---|
| Coors Field | 2010 | 136% | 150% | 122% | 128% | 168% | 92% |
| Coors Field | 2011 | 135% | 135% | 118% | 124% | 114% | 102% |
| Coors Field | 2012 | 158% | 149% | 128% | 122% | 197% | 108% |
| Coors Field | 2013 | 127% | 117% | 116% | 112% | 172% | 99% |
| Coors Field | 2014 | 150% | 139% | 132% | 122% | 190% | 105% |
| 5 Year Average | | 141% | 138% | 123% | 122% | 168% | 101% |

| Year | Over | Under | Push | Over % | Under % | RF | RA |
|---|---|---|---|---|---|---|---|
| 2010 | 44 | 36 | 1 | 55% | 45% | 5.9 | 4.7 |
| 2011 | 49 | 31 | 1 | 61% | 39% | 5.4 | 5.3 |
| 2012 | 49 | 28 | 4 | 64% | 36% | 6.0 | 6.5 |
| 2013 | 41 | 38 | 2 | 52% | 48% | 5.4 | 4.8 |
| 2014 | 43 | 34 | 4 | 56% | 44% | 6.2 | 5.5 |
| Total | 226 | 167 | 12 | 58% | 42% | 5.8 | 5.4 |

# Colorado

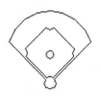

There's another rule of thumb some bettors use when handicapping the Rockies: never bet against them at home, and never bet on them on the road. History shows us that is a good plan of action. Over the past five years, the Rockies have been a disaster away from home. Colorado lost 34 units in 2014, and have lost 89 units overall since 2010.

| Year | Hm Win | Hm Loss | Win % | Units | Rd Win | Rd Loss | Win % | Units |
|------|--------|---------|-------|-------|--------|---------|-------|-------|
| 2010 | 52 | 29 | 64% | 9 | 31 | 50 | 38% | -22 |
| 2011 | 38 | 43 | 47% | -20 | 35 | 46 | 43% | -9.7 |
| 2012 | 35 | 46 | 43% | -11 | 29 | 52 | 36% | -8.4 |
| 2013 | 45 | 36 | 56% | 2 | 29 | 52 | 36% | -15 |
| 2014 | 45 | 36 | 56% | 5.9 | 21 | 60 | 26% | -34 |
| Total | 215 | 190 | 53% | -14 | 145 | 260 | 36% | -89 |

# COMERICA PARK, DETROIT

Comerica had been a hitter's park in recent years, but that trend wasn't the case in 2014. The park factor was right at league average last year. The Over still hit at 55% in the park, however, even with the drop in run scoring. A major reason for the change was the decrease in doubles; teams at Comerica hit doubles at just 80% of the major league average last year. I expect that to return to the league average, and bring the run scoring back along with it. Comerica typically increases home runs from left-handed hitters and cuts down on strikeouts. The large park and layout make triples very common.

| PARK NAME | Year | RUNS | HR | H | 2B | 3B | BB |
|---|---|---|---|---|---|---|---|
| Comerica Park | 2010 | 98% | 92% | 103% | 97% | 103% | 93% |
| Comerica Park | 2011 | 106% | 99% | 105% | 101% | 232% | 87% |
| Comerica Park | 2012 | 107% | 103% | 103% | 92% | 153% | 98% |
| Comerica Park | 2013 | 114% | 101% | 105% | 110% | 168% | 106% |
| Comerica Park | 2014 | 100% | 101% | 98% | 80% | 183% | 102% |
| 5 Year Average | | 105% | 99% | 103% | 96% | 168% | 97% |

| Year | Over | Under | Push | Over % | Under % | RF | RA |
|---|---|---|---|---|---|---|---|
| 2010 | 37 | 39 | 5 | 49% | 51% | 5.1 | 4.1 |
| 2011 | 45 | 34 | 7 | 57% | 43% | 5.0 | 4.5 |
| 2012 | 39 | 45 | 3 | 46% | 54% | 4.8 | 3.9 |
| 2013 | 48 | 32 | 6 | 60% | 40% | 5.2 | 4.1 |
| 2014 | 43 | 35 | 4 | 55% | 45% | 4.5 | 4.5 |
| Total | 212 | 185 | 25 | 53% | 47% | 4.9 | 4.2 |

# Detroit

The Tigers struggled last year on the road, but historically have been one of the better teams in the MLB at home. You do have to pay the price to bet them, however. The Tigers have lost 15 units over the last two years despite winning 59% of their games.

| Year | Hm Win | Hm Loss | Win % | Units | Rd Win | Rd Loss | Win % | Units |
|-------|--------|---------|-------|-------|--------|---------|-------|-------|
| 2010 | 52 | 29 | 64% | 17 | 29 | 52 | 36% | -20 |
| 2011 | 53 | 33 | 62% | 8.7 | 47 | 40 | 54% | 9.6 |
| 2012 | 54 | 33 | 62% | 2.8 | 41 | 47 | 47% | -15 |
| 2013 | 53 | 33 | 62% | -5.5 | 45 | 42 | 52% | -8.1 |
| 2014 | 45 | 37 | 55% | -10 | 45 | 38 | 54% | 2.8 |
| Total | 257 | 165 | 61% | 12.7 | 207 | 219 | 49% | -31 |

# MINUTE MAID PARK, HOUSTON

Minute Maid Park has a retractable roof that will typically be closed during the season. Astros players love playing with the roof closed; even on nice days, the roof remains closed. When closed, the air conditioning takes over and keeps the ball from carrying as it does on those rare occasions where it is open. The park plays small at times; home runs into the left field stands are fly-ball outs in most stadiums. The huge center field does help make up for the short fences down the corners. While both lefty and righty hitters see their power numbers inflated by the park, right-handers are able to take the most advantage. Pitchers are helped by a decrease in walks allowed and a slight increase in the number of strikeouts allowed in the park.

| PARK NAME | Year | RUNS | HR | H | 2B | 3B | BB |
|---|---|---|---|---|---|---|---|
| Minute Maid Park | 2010 | 86% | 108% | 92% | 95% | 130% | 99% |
| Minute Maid Park | 2011 | 110% | 116% | 103% | 119% | 97% | 106% |
| Minute Maid Park | 2012 | 94% | 98% | 97% | 95% | 91% | 105% |
| Minute Maid Park | 2013 | 107% | 123% | 101% | 90% | 138% | 111% |
| Minute Maid Park | 2014 | 101% | 117% | 101% | 105% | 145% | 96% |
| 5 Year Average | | 100% | 113% | 99% | 101% | 120% | 103% |

| Year | Over | Under | Push | Over % | Under % | RF | RA |
|---|---|---|---|---|---|---|---|
| 2010 | 32 | 44 | 5 | 42% | 58% | 3.7 | 4.0 |
| 2011 | 49 | 32 | 0 | 61% | 40% | 4.0 | 5.1 |
| 2012 | 36 | 40 | 5 | 47% | 53% | 3.8 | 4.4 |
| 2013 | 40 | 37 | 4 | 52% | 48% | 3.7 | 5.6 |
| 2014 | 39 | 41 | 1 | 49% | 51% | 3.9 | 4.5 |
| Total | 196 | 194 | 15 | 50% | 50% | 3.8 | 4.7 |

# Houston

The Astros were a disaster at home in 2013, losing 25 units and finished with a stunningly pathetic 24-57 home record. They rebounded nicely in 2014, winning 38 games and one unit in the process. Since 2010, Houston has lost 39 units at home and 41 units on the road.

| Year | Hm Win | Hm Loss | Win % | Units | Rd Win | Rd Loss | Win % | Units |
|------|--------|---------|-------|-------|--------|---------|-------|-------|
| 2010 | 42 | 39 | 52% | 3.1 | 34 | 47 | 42% | 7.2 |
| 2011 | 31 | 50 | 38% | -15 | 25 | 56 | 31% | -19 |
| 2012 | 35 | 46 | 43% | -3 | 20 | 61 | 25% | -28 |
| 2013 | 24 | 57 | 30% | -25 | 27 | 54 | 33% | -1.3 |
| 2014 | 38 | 43 | 47% | 1 | 32 | 49 | 40% | 0.6 |
| Total | 170 | 235 | 42% | -39 | 138 | 267 | 34% | -41 |

# KAUFFMAN STADIUM, KANSAS CITY

Kauffman Stadium was built in 1973 and is still one of the better parks in baseball. Weather effects are important here. In the springtime, the wind often comes in from the north, keeping scores down. Once the temperature heats up, however, so does the scoring. On hot days, the ball flies all over the park. Even so, it is extremely difficult to hit home runs in Kaufman. Increases in doubles and triples help make up the difference; other than a small blip in 2008, scoring is above league average. Triples were down in 2014 along with home runs; I expect that number to return to normal next season.

| PARK NAME | Year | RUNS | HR | H | 2B | 3B | BB |
|---|---|---|---|---|---|---|---|
| Kauffman Stadium | 2010 | 101% | 92% | 104% | 103% | 260% | 90% |
| Kauffman Stadium | 2011 | 99% | 71% | 101% | 101% | 140% | 110% |
| Kauffman Stadium | 2012 | 103% | 103% | 104% | 103% | 126% | 99% |
| Kauffman Stadium | 2013 | 108% | 88% | 104% | 106% | 152% | 99% |
| Kauffman Stadium | 2014 | 101% | 84% | 101% | 104% | 107% | 95% |
| 5 Year Average | | 103% | 88% | 103% | 103% | 157% | 99% |

| Year | Over | Under | Push | Over % | Under % | RF | RA |
|---|---|---|---|---|---|---|---|
| 2010 | 41 | 38 | 2 | 52% | 48% | 4.4 | 5.0 |
| 2011 | 38 | 37 | 6 | 51% | 49% | 4.6 | 4.6 |
| 2012 | 34 | 43 | 4 | 44% | 56% | 4.2 | 4.7 |
| 2013 | 31 | 44 | 6 | 41% | 59% | 4.0 | 4.0 |
| 2014 | 42 | 45 | 2 | 48% | 52% | 3.8 | 4.1 |
| Total | 186 | 207 | 20 | 47% | 53% | 4.2 | 4.5 |

# Kansas City

The Royals are a strange case. Playing in one of the great ballparks in the game, Kansas City has historically struggled at home while being profitable on the road. Last year was no exception. The Royals lost seven units at Kaufman while winning 18 units on the road. Maybe they should change the pre-game menu in Kansas City...

| Year | Hm Win | Hm Loss | Win % | Units | Rd Win | Rd Loss | Win % | Units |
|-------|--------|---------|-------|-------|--------|---------|-------|-------|
| 2010 | 38 | 43 | 47% | -2.3 | 29 | 52 | 36% | -7.5 |
| 2011 | 40 | 41 | 49% | -2.3 | 31 | 50 | 38% | -4.2 |
| 2012 | 37 | 44 | 46% | -7.1 | 35 | 46 | 43% | 2.4 |
| 2013 | 44 | 37 | 54% | -1.1 | 42 | 39 | 52% | 7.1 |
| 2014 | 48 | 41 | 54% | -7 | 52 | 36 | 59% | 18.2 |
| Total | 207 | 206 | 50% | -20 | 189 | 223 | 46% | 16 |

# ANGEL STADIUM, ANAHEIM

Angel Stadium was built in 1962 and has undergone several modifications since. Ground ball pitchers tend to do well here, and teams without a rangy center fielder can struggle covering the outfield. The right field alley is 17 feet closer to home plate than the left field alley. An 18-foot high wall in right field turns many potential home runs into loud doubles, however. The home run rate from left-handed hitters is much lower in this stadium than elsewhere. Run scoring has really fallen off in recent years; the stadium is now the most difficult scoring environment in the American League.

| PARK NAME | Year | RUNS | HR | H | 2B | 3B | BB |
|---|---|---|---|---|---|---|---|
| Angel Stadium | 2010 | 86% | 83% | 95% | 82% | 47% | 97% |
| Angel Stadium | 2011 | 84% | 79% | 94% | 86% | 64% | 96% |
| Angel Stadium | 2012 | 81% | 76% | 91% | 91% | 110% | 77% |
| Angel Stadium | 2013 | 97% | 90% | 101% | 96% | 100% | 99% |
| Angel Stadium | 2014 | 92% | 84% | 98% | 99% | 55% | 92% |
| 5 Year Average | | 88% | 82% | 96% | 91% | 75% | 92% |

| Year | Over | Under | Push | Over % | Under % | RF | RA |
|---|---|---|---|---|---|---|---|
| 2010 | 32 | 44 | 5 | 42% | 58% | 3.9 | 4.0 |
| 2011 | 29 | 42 | 10 | 41% | 59% | 3.8 | 3.5 |
| 2012 | 35 | 42 | 4 | 46% | 55% | 4.3 | 3.8 |
| 2013 | 44 | 36 | 1 | 55% | 45% | 4.3 | 4.6 |
| 2014 | 35 | 43 | 5 | 45% | 55% | 4.4 | 3.8 |
| Total | 175 | 207 | 25 | 46% | 54% | 4.1 | 3.9 |

# L.A. Angels

The Angels were equally impressive home and away in 2014, winning over eight units in each category. The home record was a nice bounce back from 2013's disaster; the Angels lost 19 units at home that season. Anaheim has always been a scrappy team and that has translated into being a strong road team as well.

| Year | Hm Win | Hm Loss | Win % | Units | Rd Win | Rd Loss | Win % | Units |
|-------|--------|---------|-------|-------|--------|---------|-------|-------|
| 2010  | 43     | 38      | 53%   | -7.9  | 37     | 44      | 46%   | -1.1  |
| 2011  | 45     | 36      | 56%   | 1.1   | 41     | 40      | 51%   | 0.1   |
| 2012  | 46     | 35      | 57%   | -9    | 43     | 38      | 53%   | -1.5  |
| 2013  | 39     | 42      | 48%   | -19   | 39     | 42      | 48%   | -2.4  |
| 2014  | 52     | 31      | 63%   | 8.3   | 46     | 36      | 56%   | 8.4   |
| Total | 225    | 182     | 55%   | -26   | 206    | 200     | 51%   | 3.5   |

# DODGER STADIUM, LOS ANGELES

Dodger Stadium, opened in 1962, is currently the third-oldest ballpark in MLB, after Fenway Park in Boston (opened in 1912) and Wrigley Field in Chicago (opened in 1914). It is the largest MLB stadium by seat capacity. Dodger Stadium is known as a pitcher's park thanks to a large foul ground that helps get pitchers out of jams. Despite the difficulty in scoring runs, the Over won 63% of the time in 2014. Home runs are relatively easy to hit in the stadium, particularly for left-handed hitters. Ground ball pitchers do well here, as do teams with power bats in their lineup.

| PARK NAME | Year | RUNS | HR | H | 2B | 3B | BB |
|---|---|---|---|---|---|---|---|
| Dodger Stadium | 2010 | 94% | 102% | 99% | 95% | 33% | 102% |
| Dodger Stadium | 2011 | 94% | 92% | 95% | 96% | 61% | 103% |
| Dodger Stadium | 2012 | 87% | 113% | 97% | 82% | 49% | 97% |
| Dodger Stadium | 2013 | 87% | 96% | 96% | 93% | 46% | 84% |
| Dodger Stadium | 2014 | 91% | 123% | 91% | 106% | 35% | 84% |
| 5 Year Average | | 90% | 105% | 95% | 94% | 45% | 94% |

| Year | Over | Under | Push | Over % | Under % | RF | RA |
|---|---|---|---|---|---|---|---|
| 2010 | 41 | 38 | 2 | 52% | 48% | 4.0 | 4.1 |
| 2011 | 37 | 36 | 8 | 51% | 49% | 3.7 | 3.8 |
| 2012 | 33 | 44 | 4 | 43% | 57% | 3.8 | 3.3 |
| 2013 | 41 | 41 | 4 | 50% | 50% | 3.6 | 3.5 |
| 2014 | 49 | 29 | 5 | 63% | 37% | 4.1 | 3.8 |
| Total | 201 | 188 | 23 | 52% | 48% | 3.8 | 3.7 |

# LA Dodgers

The Dodgers were better on the road in 2014, winning 12.8 units while losing 5.9 units at Dodger Stadium. That continues the trend over the past four season. LA routinely is in positive territory in its road games while losing money at home. Since 2010, the Dodgers at +17 in away games and -17 at home.

| Year | Hm Win | Hm Loss | Win % | Units | Rd Win | Rd Loss | Win % | Units |
|------|--------|---------|-------|-------|--------|---------|-------|-------|
| 2010 | 45 | 36 | 56% | -2.8 | 35 | 46 | 43% | -9.8 |
| 2011 | 42 | 39 | 52% | -4.5 | 40 | 40 | 50% | 5.2 |
| 2012 | 45 | 36 | 56% | -2.3 | 41 | 40 | 51% | 3.6 |
| 2013 | 51 | 35 | 59% | -1.3 | 46 | 40 | 54% | 5.3 |
| 2014 | 46 | 37 | 55% | -5.9 | 49 | 34 | 59% | 12.8 |
| Total | 229 | 183 | 56% | -17 | 211 | 200 | 51% | 17.1 |

# MARLINS PARK, MIAMI

There is a lot of wide-open space in Marlins Park. Speedy contact hitters can thrive here. It is difficult to hit home runs, and the lightning fast grass once led to a ton of triples in this park. Defense is a key here. The park is very large, and speed in the outfield will help a pitcher immensely. Fly-ball pitchers do well in this park; leaving the ball up often just results in 400-foot outs. The park has a retractable roof that is closed most of time. There can be a breeze however. Retractable glass windows can be open even if the roof is closed. The wind isn't enough to affect play, but does add a level of comfort to fans in the seats.

| PARK NAME | Year | RUNS | HR | H | 2B | 3B | BB |
|---|---|---|---|---|---|---|---|
| Sun Life | 2010 | 104% | 82% | 99% | 110% | 90% | 118% |
| Sun Life | 2011 | 99% | 94% | 99% | 98% | 124% | 115% |
| Marlins Park | 2012 | 101% | 72% | 100% | 94% | 126% | 103% |
| Marlins Park | 2013 | 103% | 64% | 101% | 114% | 132% | 104% |
| Marlins Park | 2014 | 101% | 79% | 99% | 103% | 192% | 95% |
| 3 Year Average | | 102% | 72% | 100% | 104% | 150% | 101% |

| Year | Over | Under | Push | Over % | Under % | RF | RA |
|---|---|---|---|---|---|---|---|
| 2010 | 42 | 34 | 2 | 55% | 45% | 4.4 | 4.5 |
| 2011 | 39 | 34 | 5 | 53% | 47% | 3.8 | 4.3 |
| 2012 | 42 | 34 | 5 | 55% | 45% | 3.8 | 4.5 |
| 2013 | 34 | 40 | 7 | 46% | 54% | 3.4 | 3.9 |
| 2014 | 40 | 33 | 8 | 55% | 45% | 4.3 | 3.9 |
| Total | 197 | 175 | 27 | 53% | 47% | 3.9 | 4.2 |

# Miami

The Marlins haven't set the world on fire since moving into their new stadium in 2012. Miami has lost 11.5 units while at Marlins Park. That is better than their road record, however. Miami has lost 28 units in that same period away from home.

| Year | Hm Win | Hm Loss | Win % | Units | Rd Win | Rd Loss | Win % | Units |
|------|--------|---------|-------|-------|--------|---------|-------|-------|
| 2010 | 39 | 39 | 50% | -5.6 | 41 | 43 | 49% | 3.9 |
| 2011 | 31 | 47 | 40% | -22 | 41 | 43 | 49% | 7.2 |
| 2012 | 38 | 43 | 47% | -11 | 31 | 50 | 38% | -14 |
| 2013 | 36 | 45 | 44% | -2.1 | 26 | 55 | 32% | -12 |
| 2014 | 42 | 39 | 52% | 1.6 | 35 | 46 | 43% | -1.8 |
| Total | 186 | 213 | 47% | -39 | 174 | 237 | 42% | -17 |

# MILLER PARK, MILWAUKEE

Fly-ball pitchers walk a thin line at Miller Park. Down the lines, the park is deep, but the alleys are short and hitters can take advantage. Foul ball territory is small. The roof keeps the cold out, which hitters appreciate in April and May. There is no air conditioning, but an air circulation system keeps the park 30 degrees warmer than the outside temperature. Shadows are a problem during day games; umpires and players both have complained about seeing the ball. The Brewers recently have tried manipulating the roof to minimize shadows in day games, so any change in play may not be noticeable looking at the raw numbers.

| PARK NAME | Year | RUNS | HR | H | 2B | 3B | BB |
|---|---|---|---|---|---|---|---|
| Miller Park | 2010 | 101% | 123% | 99% | 99% | 60% | 103% |
| Miller Park | 2011 | 104% | 106% | 106% | 109% | 127% | 108% |
| Miller Park | 2012 | 117% | 163% | 100% | 99% | 133% | 106% |
| Miller Park | 2013 | 111% | 126% | 108% | 104% | 107% | 117% |
| Miller Park | 2014 | 100% | 114% | 97% | 86% | 52% | 98% |
| 5 Year Average | | 107% | 127% | 102% | 99% | 96% | 106% |

| Year | Over | Under | Push | Over % | Under % | RF | RA |
|---|---|---|---|---|---|---|---|
| 2010 | 44 | 33 | 4 | 57% | 43% | 4.5 | 5.1 |
| 2011 | 45 | 38 | 4 | 54% | 46% | 4.9 | 3.9 |
| 2012 | 47 | 33 | 1 | 59% | 41% | 5.4 | 4.6 |
| 2013 | 41 | 38 | 2 | 52% | 48% | 4.0 | 4.6 |
| 2014 | 37 | 43 | 1 | 46% | 54% | 4.1 | 4.0 |
| Total | 214 | 185 | 12 | 54% | 46% | 4.6 | 4.4 |

# Milwaukee

The Brewers were better at home in 2014, but still need to get better if they hope to contend in the NL Central. Milwaukee went 37-44 at home in 2013 and 42-39 in 2014, combining for a net loss of 21 units. They were more profitable on the road, winning six units over the past two seasons.

| Year | Hm Win | Hm Loss | Win % | Units | Rd Win | Rd Loss | Win % | Units |
|------|--------|---------|-------|-------|--------|---------|-------|-------|
| 2010 | 40 | 41 | 49% | -9.5 | 37 | 44 | 46% | 2 |
| 2011 | 61 | 26 | 70% | 27.3 | 40 | 46 | 47% | -7.8 |
| 2012 | 49 | 32 | 61% | 6.8 | 34 | 47 | 42% | -17 |
| 2013 | 37 | 44 | 46% | -10 | 37 | 44 | 46% | 2.9 |
| 2014 | 42 | 39 | 52% | -11 | 40 | 41 | 49% | 3.2 |
| Total | 229 | 182 | 56% | 3.9 | 188 | 222 | 46% | -17 |

# TARGET FIELD, MINNESOTA

Target Field was expected to be a pitcher's park when it first opened in 2010. Justin Morneau said the gaps were "ridiculous" and that it is almost impossible for a right-handed hitter to hit an opposite field homer. That was true the first few years, but run scoring has been above league average the last three seasons. Lefties still have problems hitting home runs. When handicapping games, weather is a huge factor. The average April high temperature in Minneapolis is 55 degrees, not a good way for the offense to rack up high numbers. Minneapolis is also one of the windiest cities in the United States, meaning a bettor needs to pay close attention to which way the wind is blowing before making a wager on the total.

| PARK NAME | Year | RUNS | HR | H | 2B | 3B | BB |
|---|---|---|---|---|---|---|---|
| Target Field | 2010 | 96% | 64% | 100% | 110% | 117% | 106% |
| Target Field | 2011 | 94% | 91% | 101% | 93% | 94% | 96% |
| Target Field | 2012 | 104% | 103% | 103% | 99% | 191% | 108% |
| Target Field | 2013 | 102% | 80% | 103% | 112% | 105% | 84% |
| Target Field | 2014 | 112% | 102% | 108% | 108% | 141% | 108% |
| 5 Year Average | | 102% | 88% | 103% | 104% | 129% | 100% |

| Year | Over | Under | Push | Over % | Under % | RF | RA |
|---|---|---|---|---|---|---|---|
| 2010 | 40 | 40 | 3 | 50% | 50% | 4.9 | 3.9 |
| 2011 | 39 | 39 | 3 | 50% | 50% | 3.6 | 5.0 |
| 2012 | 38 | 36 | 7 | 51% | 49% | 4.5 | 5.1 |
| 2013 | 37 | 44 | 0 | 46% | 54% | 3.7 | 5.0 |
| 2014 | 47 | 30 | 4 | 61% | 39% | 4.5 | 5.2 |
| Total | 201 | 189 | 17 | 52% | 48% | 4.2 | 4.8 |

# Minnesota

The Twins have certainly made visitors feel welcome at their new ballpark. After 53-30 at home in their first season, Minnesota has struggled. Last year's 35-46 home record was the best in the past four years. The Twins have lost 60 units at home since 2010.

| Year | Hm Win | Hm Loss | Win % | Units | Rd Win | Rd Loss | Win % | Units |
|------|--------|---------|-------|-------|--------|---------|-------|-------|
| 2010 | 53 | 30 | 64% | 9.6 | 41 | 41 | 50% | 0.5 |
| 2011 | 33 | 48 | 41% | -17 | 30 | 51 | 37% | -8.2 |
| 2012 | 31 | 50 | 38% | -19 | 35 | 46 | 43% | 6 |
| 2013 | 32 | 49 | 40% | -14 | 34 | 47 | 42% | 6.8 |
| 2014 | 35 | 46 | 43% | -10 | 35 | 46 | 43% | 3.9 |
| Total | 184 | 223 | 45% | -49 | 175 | 231 | 43% | 9 |

# YANKEE STADIUM, NEW YORK

Everything is big in the new Yankee Stadium. The concourses, the seats, the huge Diamond Vision in the outfield, even the Yankee Stadium signs dominate the view. The stadium opened in 2009 with a panic from baseball purists; home runs flew out of the place at an alarming rate. Things eventually calmed down for a while, but 2014 saw the home run rate jump up again. LH power hitters especially take advantage of the small right-field fence. Right-handed hitters don't have it as easy but still have few difficulties in racking up good power numbers. Despite that, run scoring was below league average in 2014. Extra-base hits other than home runs aren't that common in the new stadium.

| PARK NAME | Year | RUNS | HR | H | 2B | 3B | BB |
|---|---|---|---|---|---|---|---|
| Yankee Stadium | 2010 | 118% | 142% | 104% | 106% | 70% | 95% |
| Yankee Stadium | 2011 | 113% | 127% | 104% | 99% | 84% | 103% |
| Yankee Stadium | 2012 | 99% | 114% | 93% | 88% | 42% | 101% |
| Yankee Stadium | 2013 | 109% | 113% | 105% | 96% | 73% | 108% |
| Yankee Stadium | 2014 | 95% | 147% | 101% | 88% | 53% | 96% |
| 5 Yr Park Factor | | 107% | 129% | 101% | 95% | 64% | 101% |

| Year | Over | Under | Push | Over % | Under % | RF | RA |
|---|---|---|---|---|---|---|---|
| 2010 | 48 | 32 | 5 | 60% | 40% | 5.8 | 4.6 |
| 2011 | 43 | 35 | 6 | 55% | 45% | 5.8 | 4.2 |
| 2012 | 35 | 50 | 1 | 41% | 59% | 4.8 | 4.0 |
| 2013 | 38 | 40 | 3 | 49% | 51% | 4.2 | 4.3 |
| 2014 | 32 | 46 | 3 | 41% | 59% | 3.8 | 4.0 |
| Total | 196 | 203 | 18 | 49% | 51% | 4.9 | 4.2 |

# New York Yankees

The Yankees have become a dull team in a dull park with a dull record. New York lost six units at home in 2014, despite finishing 43-38. They showed a little profit on the road (3.8 units). Maybe A-Rod can liven things up in 2015.

| Year | Hm Win | Hm Loss | Win % | Units | Rd Win | Rd Loss | Win % | Units |
|------|--------|---------|-------|-------|--------|---------|-------|-------|
| 2010 | 54 | 31 | 64% | -0.3 | 46 | 40 | 54% | -5.4 |
| 2011 | 53 | 31 | 63% | 4.4 | 46 | 37 | 55% | 2.6 |
| 2012 | 53 | 33 | 62% | 1.3 | 45 | 40 | 53% | -2.4 |
| 2013 | 46 | 35 | 57% | 2 | 39 | 42 | 48% | 3 |
| 2014 | 43 | 38 | 53% | -6 | 41 | 40 | 51% | 3.8 |
| Total | 249 | 168 | 60% | 1.4 | 217 | 199 | 52% | 1.6 |

# CITI FIELD, NEW YORK

Shea Stadium was always a pitcher's park, and the new stadium for the Mets is no different despite a number of modifications made to the park since it opened in 2009. Changes include building an eight-foot wall in front of the high 16-foot wall in left field that many had dubbed the "Great Wall of Flushing", removing the nook in right field, and reducing the distance in right center field from 415 feet from home plate to 390 feet. That has helped some, but run-scoring still remains low. Weather conditions and heavy sea air can't be changed with a new wall or two. Nevertheless, the power numbers are up, especially for right-handed batters, and the hope is run scoring will follow.

| PARK NAME | Year | RUNS | HR | H | 2B | 3B | BB |
|---|---|---|---|---|---|---|---|
| City Field | 2010 | 89% | 72% | 93% | 87% | 131% | 110% |
| Citi Field | 2011 | 91% | 74% | 96% | 97% | 121% | 104% |
| City Field | 2012 | 87% | 107% | 92% | 79% | 63% | 97% |
| Citi Field | 2013 | 87% | 112% | 89% | 84% | 70% | 103% |
| Citi Field | 2014 | 85% | 96% | 92% | 104% | 67% | 98% |
| 5 Yr. Park factor | | 87% | 97% | 92% | 91% | 80% | 100% |

| Year | Over | Under | Push | Over % | Under % | RF | RA |
|---|---|---|---|---|---|---|---|
| 2010 | 34 | 45 | 2 | 43% | 57% | 4.1 | 3.5 |
| 2011 | 43 | 35 | 3 | 55% | 45% | 4.0 | 4.5 |
| 2012 | 37 | 40 | 4 | 48% | 52% | 3.5 | 4.3 |
| 2013 | 37 | 43 | 1 | 46% | 54% | 3.3 | 4.2 |
| 2014 | 34 | 41 | 6 | 45% | 55% | 3.5 | 3.5 |
| Total | 185 | 204 | 16 | 48% | 52% | 3.7 | 4.0 |

# New York Mets

The Mets have been better on the road over the past five years, a tricky accomplishment to achieve in today's game. It's not that the Mets are horrible, however. It is more that they have been solid on the road. New York has won 48% of its road games, a number most teams would gladly have. The problem is they've won only 47% of their home games at the same time. Down 50 units at home, and +29.6 on the road...hmmmm.

| Year | Hm Win | Hm Loss | Win % | Units | Rd Win | Rd Loss | Win % | Units |
|-------|--------|---------|-------|-------|--------|---------|-------|-------|
| 2010  | 47     | 34      | 58%   | 7.2   | 32     | 49      | 40%   | -13   |
| 2011  | 34     | 47      | 42%   | -18   | 43     | 38      | 53%   | 17.5  |
| 2012  | 36     | 45      | 44%   | -17   | 38     | 43      | 47%   | 3.7   |
| 2013  | 33     | 48      | 41%   | -20   | 41     | 40      | 51%   | 17    |
| 2014  | 40     | 41      | 49%   | -1.7  | 39     | 42      | 48%   | 4.8   |
| Total | 190    | 215     | 47%   | -50   | 193    | 212     | 48%   | 29.6  |

# OAKLAND COLISEUM, OAKLAND

Oakland is a park that plays differently at night than it does during the day: Lower scoring at night, higher scoring during the day. When the weather heats up during the summer, the ball carries well. When it is damp and wet, run scoring decreases. The foul grounds are huge and the infield tends to be quick; a team that has speed on defense can do well here. Overall, it is a pitcher's park. It is extremely difficult to hit home runs in the park, especially for left-handed batters.

| PARK NAME | Year | RUNS | HR | H | 2B | 3B | BB |
|---|---|---|---|---|---|---|---|
| Oakland Coliseum | 2010 | 96% | 70% | 92% | 90% | 147% | 99% |
| Oakland Coliseum | 2011 | 95% | 79% | 93% | 97% | 90% | 106% |
| Oakland Coliseum | 2012 | 89% | 86% | 93% | 84% | 109% | 102% |
| Oakland Coliseum | 2013 | 89% | 82% | 98% | 111% | 132% | 104% |
| Oakland Coliseum | 2014 | 102% | 90% | 102% | 111% | 120% | 105% |
| 5 Year Average | | 94% | 81% | 96% | 99% | 120% | 103% |

| Year | Over | Under | Push | Over % | Under % | RF | RA |
|---|---|---|---|---|---|---|---|
| 2010 | 33 | 43 | 5 | 43% | 57% | 4.4 | 3.4 |
| 2011 | 43 | 30 | 8 | 59% | 41% | 4.1 | 3.8 |
| 2012 | 35 | 45 | 2 | 44% | 56% | 4.2 | 3.5 |
| 2013 | 40 | 43 | 1 | 48% | 52% | 4.2 | 3.7 |
| 2014 | 42 | 38 | 1 | 53% | 48% | 4.6 | 3.5 |
| Total | 193 | 199 | 17 | 49% | 51% | 4.3 | 3.6 |

# Oakland

The A's have been dominant in Oakland over the past few seasons, winning 25 units since the start of the 2010 season. The sewage problems and other difficulties with the Coliseum might be Billy Beane's new discovery in market inefficiency. Rule of thumb: look twice before betting against Oakland at home.

| Year | Hm Win | Hm Loss | Win % | Units | Rd Win | Rd Loss | Win % | Units |
|------|--------|---------|-------|-------|--------|---------|-------|-------|
| 2010 | 47 | 34 | 58% | 8.1 | 34 | 47 | 42% | -9.3 |
| 2011 | 43 | 38 | 53% | -4 | 31 | 50 | 38% | -12 |
| 2012 | 51 | 31 | 62% | 20.6 | 45 | 40 | 53% | 15.9 |
| 2013 | 53 | 31 | 63% | 8.8 | 45 | 38 | 54% | 9.4 |
| 2014 | 48 | 33 | 59% | -8 | 40 | 42 | 49% | -9.5 |
| Total | 242 | 167 | 59% | 25.5 | 195 | 217 | 47% | -5.9 |

# CITIZENS BANK PARK, PHILADELPHIA

Since opening in 2004, Citizens Bank Park has earned a reputation as one of the better power hitting parks in baseball. That hasn't translated into a high-scoring environment, however. The park plays near league average in most years. When the weather is hot, the ball flies out of the park.

| PARK NAME | Year | RUNS | HR | H | 2B | 3B | BB |
|---|---|---|---|---|---|---|---|
| Citizens Bank Park | 2010 | 99% | 113% | 98% | 99% | 87% | 95% |
| Citizens Bank Park | 2011 | 100% | 95% | 97% | 102% | 81% | 102% |
| Citizens Bank Park | 2012 | 97% | 109% | 95% | 99% | 71% | 108% |
| Citizens Bank Park | 2013 | 111% | 152% | 99% | 105% | 106% | 104% |
| Citizens Bank Park | 2014 | 93% | 121% | 97% | 91% | 84% | 100% |
| 5 Year Average | | 100% | 118% | 97% | 99% | 86% | 102% |

| Year | Over | Under | Push | Over % | Under % | RF | RA |
|---|---|---|---|---|---|---|---|
| 2010 | 38 | 45 | 3 | 46% | 54% | 4.8 | 3.8 |
| 2011 | 39 | 40 | 5 | 49% | 51% | 4.5 | 3.2 |
| 2012 | 41 | 35 | 5 | 54% | 46% | 4.0 | 4.3 |
| 2013 | 43 | 34 | 4 | 56% | 44% | 4.2 | 4.6 |
| 2014 | 39 | 35 | 7 | 53% | 47% | 3.7 | 4.0 |
| Total | 200 | 189 | 24 | 51% | 49% | 4.2 | 4.0 |

# Philadelphia

The Phillies have had a rough time of it since winning 102 games in 2011. Philadelphia has lost 42 units in the three seasons since, including 26 units at home. The Phillies historically haven't had a great home field advantage; that is more a case of playing strong on the road than not performing at home.

| Year | Hm Win | Hm Loss | Win % | Units | Rd Win | Rd Loss | Win % | Units |
|-------|--------|---------|-------|-------|--------|---------|-------|-------|
| 2010 | 55 | 31 | 64% | 3.5 | 47 | 38 | 55% | 5 |
| 2011 | 53 | 31 | 63% | 0.8 | 51 | 32 | 61% | 8.3 |
| 2012 | 40 | 41 | 49% | -15 | 41 | 40 | 51% | -1.6 |
| 2013 | 43 | 38 | 53% | -2.2 | 30 | 51 | 37% | -19 |
| 2014 | 37 | 44 | 46% | -9 | 36 | 45 | 44% | 4.7 |
| Total | 228 | 185 | 55% | -22 | 205 | 206 | 50% | -2.4 |

# PNC PARK, PITTSBURGH

PNC was initially a neutral scoring park when it first opened. However, it is now a stadium favoring the pitcher. Fly ball pitchers are helped by the difficulty of hitting home runs in the stadium, particularly out to left field where the dimensions are much bigger than right field. Right-handers really have a tough time hitting the ball out of the park. The infield is a bit rough; a lot of errors are made at PNC compared to other National League parks. In general, one should look at playing Under at PNC Park.

| PARK NAME | Year | RUNS | HR | H | 2B | 3B | BB |
|---|---|---|---|---|---|---|---|
| PNC Park | 2010 | 103% | 80% | 99% | 112% | 130% | 99% |
| PNC Park | 2011 | 96% | 80% | 99% | 101% | 73% | 88% |
| PNC Park | 2012 | 76% | 63% | 87% | 104% | 72% | 80% |
| PNC Park | 2013 | 91% | 68% | 99% | 86% | 69% | 88% |
| PNC Park | 2014 | 98% | 71% | 104% | 108% | 81% | 99% |
| 5 Year Average | | 93% | 72% | 98% | 102% | 85% | 91% |

| Year | Over | Under | Push | Over % | Under % | RF | RA |
|---|---|---|---|---|---|---|---|
| 2010 | 39 | 39 | 3 | 50% | 50% | 4.1 | 5.0 |
| 2011 | 41 | 38 | 2 | 52% | 48% | 3.5 | 4.4 |
| 2012 | 29 | 49 | 3 | 37% | 63% | 3.7 | 3.4 |
| 2013 | 34 | 46 | 4 | 43% | 58% | 3.8 | 3.3 |
| 2014 | 36 | 40 | 6 | 47% | 53% | 4.3 | 3.7 |
| Total | 179 | 212 | 18 | 46% | 54% | 3.9 | 4.0 |

# Pittsburgh

The Pirates have been dominant at home over the past three seasons, going 148-99 and winning 27 units in the process. That isn't the case on the road, however. Pittsburgh went 116-130 (-2 units) away from PNC Park since the start of the 2011 season; last year's poor performance cost the Pirates the division.

| Year | Hm Win | Hm Loss | Win % | Units | Rd Win | Rd Loss | Win % | Units |
|-------|--------|---------|-------|-------|--------|---------|-------|-------|
| 2010 | 40 | 41 | 49% | 10 | 17 | 64 | 21% | -33 |
| 2011 | 36 | 45 | 44% | -7.9 | 36 | 45 | 44% | 6.4 |
| 2012 | 45 | 36 | 56% | 3.4 | 34 | 47 | 42% | -6.5 |
| 2013 | 52 | 32 | 62% | 11.9 | 45 | 39 | 54% | 12 |
| 2014 | 51 | 31 | 62% | 12 | 37 | 44 | 46% | -7.4 |
| Total | 224 | 185 | 55% | 29.4 | 169 | 239 | 41% | -28 |

# PETCO PARK, SAN DIEGO

In a perfect world, the prevailing San Diego winds to right field would help hitters overcome the high right field wall at Petco Field. Hitters were also going to be helped by a lower left field wall and smaller foul grounds. It didn't work out that way. Petco is a pitcher's paradise. Fly-ball pitchers do well here, as do teams with quick outfielders. The Padres have tried to change this. After the 2012 season, the left-center field wall was moved in from 402 feet to 390 feet, the right-center field wall was moved from 402 feet to 391 feet, and the right field wall was moved in from 360 feet to 349 feet. The right field wall was also lowered from eleven feet to eight feet. Home runs increased in 2013, but sunk back down to normal in 2014. What Coors Field is for hitters, Petco Park is for pitchers. Remember that when San Diego goes on the road.

| PARK NAME | Year | RUNS | HR | H | 2B | 3B | BB |
|---|---|---|---|---|---|---|---|
| Petco Park | 2010 | 88% | 86% | 90% | 81% | 130% | 113% |
| Petco Park | 2011 | 82% | 86% | 88% | 90% | 139% | 101% |
| Petco Park | 2012 | 85% | 63% | 96% | 97% | 126% | 100% |
| Petco Park | 2013 | 83% | 94% | 90% | 77% | 113% | 100% |
| Petco Park | 2014 | 83% | 81% | 92% | 91% | 96% | 106% |
| 5 Year Average | | 84% | 82% | 91% | 87% | 121% | 104% |

| Year | Over | Under | Push | Over % | Under % | RF | RA |
|---|---|---|---|---|---|---|---|
| 2010 | 36 | 39 | 6 | 48% | 52% | 4.0 | 3.2 |
| 2011 | 41 | 37 | 3 | 53% | 47% | 3.1 | 3.5 |
| 2012 | 42 | 38 | 1 | 53% | 48% | 3.8 | 3.9 |
| 2013 | 35 | 42 | 4 | 46% | 55% | 3.6 | 3.8 |
| 2014 | 31 | 47 | 3 | 40% | 60% | 3.3 | 2.9 |
| Total | 185 | 203 | 17 | 48% | 52% | 3.6 | 3.5 |

# San Diego

Oh my. A team that goes 48-33 at home shouldn't be worrying about finishing below .500. That wasn't the case last year for the Padres, thanks to a pathetic road performance. San Diego lost 20 units away from home in 2014, while winning 10.9 units at home. That's been the pattern lately, although 2014 was a bit extreme.

| Year | Hm Win | Hm Loss | Win % | Units | Rd Win | Rd Loss | Win % | Units |
|------|--------|---------|-------|-------|--------|---------|-------|-------|
| 2010 | 45 | 36 | 56% | 1.8 | 45 | 36 | 56% | 16.7 |
| 2011 | 35 | 46 | 43% | -14 | 36 | 45 | 44% | 1.9 |
| 2012 | 42 | 39 | 52% | 4.9 | 34 | 47 | 42% | -0.6 |
| 2013 | 45 | 36 | 56% | 9.6 | 31 | 50 | 38% | -6.6 |
| 2014 | 48 | 33 | 59% | 10.9 | 29 | 52 | 36% | -20 |
| Total | 215 | 190 | 53% | 13.1 | 175 | 230 | 43% | -8.8 |

# SAFECO FIELD, SEATTLE

Safeco Field has earned a solid reputation as a fabulous place to pitch. Seattle is located at sea level, and has a dense, humid climate that makes it difficult to hit for a lot of power. The grounds are also huge, particularly to the left field gap where power hitters earn their money. Left-handed hitters have done OK at Safeco the last few years. Right-handed bats have struggled. The constant rains may play a role as well. Safeco Field is unique in the fact that the roof only covers the field. The sides are open, allowing wind to play a role even if the roof is "closed". A closed roof may help funnel the western wind out to right field, pushing fly balls to right field out of the park while pushing fly balls to left field toward the deeper center field area

| PARK NAME | Year | RUNS | HR | H | 2B | 3B | BB |
|---|---|---|---|---|---|---|---|
| Safeco Field | 2010 | 81% | 68% | 93% | 92% | 65% | 102% |
| Safeco Field | 2011 | 86% | 104% | 89% | 77% | 65% | 105% |
| Safeco Field | 2012 | 69% | 58% | 83% | 71% | 53% | 100% |
| Safeco Field | 2013 | 99% | 89% | 101% | 111% | 63% | 95% |
| Safeco Field | 2014 | 83% | 105% | 89% | 79% | 47% | 88% |
| 5 Year Average | | 83% | 85% | 91% | 86% | 59% | 98% |

| Year | Over | Under | Push | Over % | Under % | RF | RA |
|---|---|---|---|---|---|---|---|
| 2010 | 28 | 50 | 3 | 36% | 64% | 3.0 | 3.8 |
| 2011 | 32 | 44 | 5 | 42% | 58% | 3.2 | 3.9 |
| 2012 | 30 | 46 | 5 | 40% | 61% | 3.2 | 3.2 |
| 2013 | 43 | 35 | 3 | 55% | 45% | 3.8 | 4.6 |
| 2014 | 26 | 49 | 6 | 35% | 65% | 3.5 | 3.2 |
| Total | 159 | 224 | 22 | 42% | 58% | 3.3 | 3.7 |

# Seattle

On the surface, the Mariners would seem to be a natural to have a strong home field advantage. A tough plane ride to Seattle and a park with unique characteristics certainly can make things difficult on road teams. That hasn't been the case, however. Seattle's poor home record cost the team a wild-card spot in 2014, and its backers 11 units as well. On the road, the Mariners won 15.4 units while winning 57% of its games.

| Year | Hm Win | Hm Loss | Win % | Units | Rd Win | Rd Loss | Win % | Units |
|------|--------|---------|-------|-------|--------|---------|-------|-------|
| 2010 | 35 | 46 | 43% | -14 | 26 | 55 | 32% | -23 |
| 2011 | 37 | 44 | 46% | -6.8 | 30 | 51 | 37% | -16 |
| 2012 | 40 | 41 | 49% | -1.3 | 35 | 46 | 43% | 4.4 |
| 2013 | 36 | 45 | 44% | -16 | 35 | 46 | 43% | 0.4 |
| 2014 | 41 | 40 | 51% | -11 | 46 | 35 | 57% | 15.4 |
| Total | 189 | 216 | 47% | -50 | 172 | 233 | 42% | -19 |

# AT&T PARK, SAN FRANCISCO

Left-handed power hitters have a horrible time pulling the ball out to right field. While McCovey Cove in right field may be reachable to some, the power alley in right center field is a killer. The deepest part in RCF is 421 away from home plate, cutting the home runs in that part of the field down to half the rate expected from a typical stadium. While home runs are depressed in this park, doubles and triples usually try to make up for it. Fly ball pitchers do well here for obvious reasons.

| PARK NAME | Year | RUNS | HR | H | 2B | 3B | BB |
|---|---|---|---|---|---|---|---|
| AT&T Park | 2010 | 94% | 89% | 97% | 98% | 84% | 99% |
| AT&T Park | 2011 | 74% | 60% | 94% | 100% | 104% | 90% |
| AT&T Park | 2012 | 74% | 52% | 90% | 89% | 81% | 102% |
| AT&T Park | 2013 | 87% | 77% | 96% | 102% | 195% | 110% |
| AT&T Park | 2014 | 92% | 68% | 95% | 92% | 181% | 99% |
| 5 Year Average | | 84% | 69% | 95% | 96% | 129% | 100% |

| Year | Over | Under | Push | Over % | Under % | RF | RA |
|---|---|---|---|---|---|---|---|
| 2010 | 37 | 45 | 6 | 45% | 55% | 4.4 | 3.4 |
| 2011 | 30 | 48 | 3 | 39% | 62% | 2.9 | 3.1 |
| 2012 | 42 | 42 | 5 | 50% | 50% | 3.9 | 3.3 |
| 2013 | 36 | 39 | 6 | 48% | 52% | 3.5 | 4.1 |
| 2014 | 42 | 43 | 4 | 49% | 51% | 4.1 | 3.5 |
| Total | 187 | 217 | 24 | 46% | 54% | 3.8 | 3.5 |

# San Francisco

The Giants have taken care of business both at home and on the road in recent years, winning three World Series in the process. At home, they are solid. On the road, they are a little bit better than solid. San Francisco has won 34.2 units in road games since the 2010 season.

| Year | Hm Win | Hm Loss | Win % | Units | Rd Win | Rd Loss | Win % | Units |
|-------|--------|---------|-------|-------|--------|---------|-------|-------|
| 2010 | 54 | 34 | 61% | 9.1 | 49 | 40 | 55% | 13.7 |
| 2011 | 46 | 35 | 57% | -2.1 | 40 | 41 | 49% | -3.3 |
| 2012 | 53 | 36 | 60% | 7.2 | 52 | 37 | 58% | 19.7 |
| 2013 | 41 | 40 | 51% | -12 | 35 | 46 | 43% | -9.3 |
| 2014 | 51 | 38 | 57% | 3.7 | 49 | 41 | 54% | 13.4 |
| Total | 245 | 183 | 57% | 6.3 | 225 | 205 | 52% | 34.2 |

# BUSCH STADIUM, ST. LOUIS

It isn't easy to describe anything costing $346 million as utilitarian, but that's what it is. First opened in 2006, the new Busch Stadium wasn't supposed to play much differently from the old Busch Stadium. For the most part, it hasn't. There are better views of the Arch and downtown, and fewer home runs being hit, but the run scoring is down only slightly. Right-handed hitters in particular have difficulties hitting home runs in Busch. Run scoring, below league average in previous seasons, took a jump in 2014. Despite that, the Over still lagged behind the Under for the year. I expect 2014 to be a fluke and the low run-scoring environment of previous seasons to return in 2015.

| PARK NAME | Year | RUNS | HR | H | 2B | 3B | BB |
|---|---|---|---|---|---|---|---|
| Busch Stadium | 2010 | 94% | 76% | 96% | 93% | 100% | 108% |
| Busch Stadium | 2011 | 90% | 77% | 88% | 81% | 63% | 101% |
| Busch Stadium | 2012 | 99% | 92% | 105% | 114% | 82% | 95% |
| Busch Stadium | 2013 | 89% | 84% | 93% | 87% | 75% | 90% |
| Busch Stadium | 2014 | 110% | 97% | 101% | 119% | 147% | 109% |
| 5 Year Average | | 96% | 85% | 96% | 99% | 93% | 100% |

| Year | Over | Under | Push | Over % | Under % | RF | RA |
|---|---|---|---|---|---|---|---|
| 2010 | 31 | 43 | 7 | 42% | 58% | 4.8 | 3.5 |
| 2011 | 43 | 44 | 3 | 49% | 51% | 4.3 | 4.1 |
| 2012 | 42 | 40 | 4 | 51% | 49% | 5.0 | 3.6 |
| 2013 | 39 | 46 | 5 | 46% | 54% | 4.6 | 3.3 |
| 2014 | 40 | 42 | 3 | 49% | 51% | 4.0 | 3.7 |
| Total | 195 | 215 | 22 | 48% | 52% | 4.5 | 3.6 |

# St. Louis

The Cardinals are extremely tough at home, yet not so hot on the road. It works, however. The Cardinals have dominated the NL Central in recent years.

| Year | Hm Win | Hm Loss | Win % | Units | Rd Win | Rd Loss | Win % | Units |
|------|--------|---------|-------|-------|--------|---------|-------|-------|
| 2010 | 52 | 29 | 64% | 1.7 | 34 | 47 | 42% | -23 |
| 2011 | 51 | 39 | 57% | -4.7 | 50 | 40 | 56% | 11.9 |
| 2012 | 53 | 33 | 62% | 5.8 | 42 | 47 | 47% | -9.9 |
| 2013 | 60 | 30 | 67% | 14.2 | 46 | 43 | 52% | -1.9 |
| 2014 | 54 | 31 | 64% | 11.5 | 40 | 46 | 47% | -9.4 |
| Total | 270 | 162 | 63% | 28.5 | 212 | 223 | 49% | -32 |

# TROPICANA FIELD, TAMPA BAY

Tropicana Field is one of those ballparks where the less said the better. The turf is incredibly fast and the ball doesn't carry well, so fly ball pitchers with fast outfielders do well here. There are many triples here due to the crazy design of the stadium walls. Home runs and doubles are lower than league average, especially in 2014. The ballpark had trended towards the Under in recent years but looks to have leveled off. Left-handed hitters can struggle here.

| PARK NAME | Year | RUNS | HR | H | 2B | 3B | BB |
|---|---|---|---|---|---|---|---|
| Tropicana Field | 2010 | 80% | 94% | 91% | 83% | 137% | 96% |
| Tropicana Field | 2011 | 82% | 90% | 92% | 85% | 72% | 96% |
| Tropicana Field | 2012 | 87% | 77% | 91% | 92% | 129% | 100% |
| Tropicana Field | 2013 | 93% | 98% | 96% | 90% | 167% | 97% |
| Tropicana Field | 2014 | 100% | 81% | 97% | 88% | 68% | 111% |
| 5 Year Average | | 88% | 88% | 93% | 88% | 114% | 100% |

| Year | Over | Under | Push | Over % | Under % | RF | RA |
|---|---|---|---|---|---|---|---|
| 2010 | 30 | 51 | 3 | 37% | 63% | 4.2 | 3.7 |
| 2011 | 26 | 52 | 5 | 33% | 67% | 3.8 | 3.5 |
| 2012 | 29 | 49 | 3 | 37% | 63% | 4.1 | 3.3 |
| 2013 | 39 | 40 | 4 | 49% | 51% | 4.2 | 3.7 |
| 2014 | 38 | 39 | 4 | 49% | 51% | 3.9 | 3.7 |
| Total | 162 | 231 | 19 | 41% | 59% | 4.0 | 3.6 |

# Tampa Bay

What happened to the Rays in 2014? Tampa has been one of the stronger home teams in baseball, even when awful. The roof fell in on them in 2014, however. Tampa lost 26 units at home last year, while finishing above .500 on the road.

| Year | Hm Win | Hm Loss | Win % | Units | Rd Win | Rd Loss | Win % | Units |
|------|--------|---------|-------|-------|--------|---------|-------|-------|
| 2010 | 49 | 35 | 58% | -9.7 | 49 | 34 | 59% | 9 |
| 2011 | 47 | 36 | 57% | -2.5 | 45 | 38 | 54% | 8.5 |
| 2012 | 46 | 35 | 57% | -4.8 | 44 | 37 | 54% | 9.4 |
| 2013 | 52 | 31 | 63% | 6.4 | 42 | 43 | 49% | -6.9 |
| 2014 | 36 | 45 | 44% | -26 | 41 | 40 | 51% | -0.7 |
| Total | 230 | 182 | 56% | -37 | 221 | 192 | 54% | 19.3 |

# THE BALLPARK, TEXAS

Coors Field East is what The Ballpark in Arlington was once called. It had been one of the best hitting environments in the game. Run scoring took a dive in 2013 and rebounded only slightly in 2014. The drop in power numbers seems to have been the cause; home runs have been hit below league average the last two seasons. The Ballpark was built with the summer wind in mind. The field is 22 feet below street level. A 42-foot high windscreen is on top of the office complex in centerfield to slow the wind down as well. In the past, wind blowing in from right field would swirl around and go back out to left, creating a nice jet-stream effect for right-handed hitters. That effect seems to have died down, possibly due to structural changes in the seating section behind home plate. Fly-ball pitchers get hammered in the Ballpark. Left-handed hitters love it here.

| PARK NAME | Year | RUNS | HR | H | 2B | 3B | BB |
|---|---|---|---|---|---|---|---|
| Rangers Ballpark | 2010 | 109% | 116% | 107% | 107% | 77% | 99% |
| Rangers Ballpark | 2011 | 141% | 150% | 113% | 119% | 233% | 103% |
| Rangers Ballpark | 2012 | 118% | 117% | 112% | 116% | 103% | 100% |
| Rangers Ballpark | 2013 | 99% | 90% | 99% | 88% | 67% | 111% |
| Rangers Ballpark | 2014 | 105% | 96% | 98% | 80% | 217% | 97% |
| 5 Year Average | | 114% | 114% | 106% | 102% | 139% | 102% |

| Year | Over | Under | Push | Over % | Under % | RF | RA |
|---|---|---|---|---|---|---|---|
| 2010 | 41 | 41 | 7 | 50% | 50% | 5.1 | 4.1 |
| 2011 | 55 | 32 | 2 | 63% | 37% | 6.1 | 5.0 |
| 2012 | 38 | 41 | 3 | 48% | 52% | 5.5 | 4.6 |
| 2013 | 29 | 49 | 4 | 37% | 63% | 4.6 | 3.8 |
| 2014 | 32 | 43 | 6 | 43% | 57% | 3.7 | 5.2 |
| Total | 195 | 206 | 22 | 49% | 51% | 5.0 | 4.5 |

# Texas

Texas hasn't had much of a home field advantage in recent years, losing money at home in four of the last five years. The problem, even before 2014's meltdown, was that the Rangers were priced high at home while winning 60% of their games. They tend to do better on the road, showing a slight cumulative profit since 2010.

| Year | Hm Win | Hm Loss | Win % | Units | Rd Win | Rd Loss | Win % | Units |
|-------|--------|---------|-------|-------|--------|---------|-------|-------|
| 2010 | 54 | 35 | 61% | -1.8 | 44 | 45 | 49% | -1.9 |
| 2011 | 58 | 31 | 65% | 10 | 48 | 42 | 53% | 2.8 |
| 2012 | 50 | 32 | 61% | -2.3 | 43 | 38 | 53% | -4.4 |
| 2013 | 46 | 36 | 56% | -12 | 45 | 36 | 56% | 7 |
| 2014 | 33 | 48 | 41% | -17 | 34 | 47 | 42% | -2.2 |
| Total | 241 | 182 | 57% | -23 | 214 | 208 | 51% | 1.3 |

# ROGERS CENTRE, TORONTO

Known as Skydome from its opening in 1989 until 2005, the Rogers Centre was the first park to draw more than four million fans. It is 31 stories high, and was the site of the first World Series game played outside of the United States. When it is closed, the power numbers are slightly down. While power hitters overall are helped by Rogers Centre, righties who can pull the ball thrive here. So do outfielders who can track down fly balls; the deep alleys place a premium on speed in the outfield.

| PARK NAME | Year | RUNS | HR | H | 2B | 3B | BB |
|---|---|---|---|---|---|---|---|
| Rogers Centre | 2010 | 106% | 136% | 103% | 93% | 108% | 95% |
| Rogers Centre | 2011 | 115% | 119% | 112% | 133% | 168% | 99% |
| Rogers Centre | 2012 | 101% | 103% | 99% | 108% | 131% | 91% |
| Rogers Centre | 2013 | 112% | 129% | 103% | 148% | 53% | 110% |
| Rogers Centre | 2014 | 104% | 131% | 103% | 111% | 133% | 92% |
| 5 Year Average | | 108% | 123% | 104% | 118% | 119% | 97% |

| Year | Over | Under | Push | Over % | Under % | RF | RA |
|---|---|---|---|---|---|---|---|
| 2010 | 40 | 36 | 5 | 53% | 47% | 4.9 | 4.6 |
| 2011 | 47 | 32 | 2 | 60% | 41% | 4.8 | 5.2 |
| 2012 | 40 | 37 | 4 | 52% | 48% | 4.5 | 4.8 |
| 2013 | 40 | 38 | 3 | 51% | 49% | 4.7 | 4.9 |
| 2014 | 38 | 40 | 3 | 49% | 51% | 4.8 | 4.1 |
| Total | 205 | 183 | 17 | 53% | 47% | 4.7 | 4.7 |

# Toronto

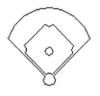

The Blue Jays had been a consistent home team, but struggled since the 2011 season. They turned it around a bit last year, winning 4.6 units and going 46-35 at home. Their road performance needs some help, however. Toronto has lost money on the road for the past three seasons.

| Year | Hm Win | Hm Loss | Win % | Units | Rd Win | Rd Loss | Win % | Units |
|-------|--------|---------|-------|-------|--------|---------|-------|-------|
| 2010 | 46 | 35 | 57% | 8.7 | 39 | 42 | 48% | 5 |
| 2011 | 42 | 39 | 52% | -1.6 | 39 | 42 | 48% | 3.5 |
| 2012 | 41 | 40 | 51% | -2.9 | 32 | 49 | 40% | -10 |
| 2013 | 40 | 41 | 49% | -7 | 34 | 47 | 42% | -3.8 |
| 2014 | 46 | 35 | 57% | 4.6 | 37 | 44 | 46% | -3.3 |
| Total | 215 | 190 | 53% | 1.8 | 181 | 224 | 45% | -8.7 |

# NATIONALS PARK, WASHINGTON

Nationals Park has been opened for seven years now, and it looks like it is a perfectly neutral ballpark. Lefty hitters have a tough time hitting it out; a 14-foot wall in right center field deserves part of the blame. Right-handed hitters also have problems hitting it out. The park does help a batter's batting average, however.

| PARK NAME | Year | RUNS | HR | H | 2B | 3B | BB |
|---|---|---|---|---|---|---|---|
| Nationals Park | 2010 | 97% | 100% | 103% | 107% | 78% | 96% |
| Nationals Park | 2011 | 96% | 111% | 103% | 100% | 68% | 75% |
| Nationals Park | 2012 | 102% | 104% | 106% | 100% | 119% | 94% |
| Nationals Park | 2013 | 101% | 80% | 109% | 105% | 58% | 97% |
| Nationals Park | 2014 | 107% | 70% | 108% | 113% | 38% | 108% |
| 5 Year Average | | 100% | 93% | 106% | 105% | 72% | 94% |

| Year | Over | Under | Push | Over % | Under % | RF | RA |
|---|---|---|---|---|---|---|---|
| 2010 | 36 | 43 | 2 | 46% | 54% | 4.0 | 4.4 |
| 2011 | 39 | 39 | 2 | 50% | 50% | 3.9 | 3.8 |
| 2012 | 42 | 37 | 5 | 53% | 47% | 4.5 | 3.8 |
| 2013 | 40 | 37 | 4 | 52% | 48% | 4.3 | 3.7 |
| 2014 | 41 | 35 | 7 | 54% | 46% | 4.4 | 3.4 |
| Total | 198 | 191 | 20 | 51% | 49% | 4.2 | 3.8 |

# Washington

The Nationals have been able to hold their own at home, winning 1.7 units last year despite having some heavy money lines in their favor. Washington continued their strong road performance as well, at least until the playoffs hit. The Nationals allowed just nine runs in four games to the Giants, yet lost three of the four games. Baseball is a funny game sometimes.

| Year | Hm Win | Hm Loss | Win % | Units | Rd Win | Rd Loss | Win % | Units |
|-------|--------|---------|-------|-------|--------|---------|-------|-------|
| 2010 | 41 | 40 | 51% | 2 | 28 | 53 | 35% | -11 |
| 2011 | 44 | 36 | 55% | 6.5 | 36 | 45 | 44% | 4.3 |
| 2012 | 51 | 33 | 61% | 7.2 | 49 | 34 | 59% | 14.4 |
| 2013 | 47 | 34 | 58% | -3.4 | 39 | 42 | 48% | -3.5 |
| 2014 | 51 | 32 | 61% | 1.7 | 46 | 37 | 55% | 4.7 |
| Total | 234 | 175 | 57% | 14 | 198 | 211 | 48% | 8.8 |

# REFERENCES AND OTHER RESOURCES

This book is just a beginning for baseball bettors. To turn a consistent profit, a bettor has to continually build on his knowledge. The following books and websites have provided much of the source material for this book, and offer additional information that will go a long way towards turning a novice bettor into a winner.

Antifragile (Nassim Nicholas Taleb)
Baseball Hacks (Joseph Adler)
Beyond Batting Average (Lee Panas)
Bill James Baseball Abstracts (Bill James)
The Book (Tom Tango, Mitchel Lichtman and Andrew Dolphin)
Fooled by Randomness (Nassim Nicholas Taleb)
Gambling Wizards: Conversations with the World's Greatest Gamblers (Richard Munchkin)
The Hidden Game of Baseball (John Thorn and Pete Palmer)
Market Wizards: Interviews with top traders (Jack D. Schwager)
Mathletics (Wayne Winston)
Moneyball (Michael Lewis)
Sharp Sports Betting (Stanford Wong)
The Signal and the Noise (Nate Silver)
Success Equation: Untangling Skill and Luck in Business, Sports and Investing (Michael Mauboussin)
Thinking, Fast and Slow (Daniel Kahneman)
Weighing the Odds in Sports Betting (King Yao)

**Websites:**

Fangraphs.com
BaseballProspectus.com
BaseballThinkFactory.org
BillJamesOnline.com
BaseballReference.com
HardballTimes.com

Retrosheet.org
TangoTiger.com
BaseballMusings.com
BaseballHQ.com
SportsOptions.com
PhilBirnbaum.com

CPSIA information can be obtained at www.ICGtesting.com
Printed in the USA
BVOW06s2213140316

439670BV00016B/205/P